Nickel Creek Why Sh...

Music transcriptions by Pete Billmann and Jeff Story

ISBN 1-4234-0233-2

7777 W. BLUEMOUND RD. P.O. BOX 13819 MILWAUKEE, WI 53213

Visit Hal Leonard Online at
www.halleonard.com

When in Rome

Words and Music by Chris Thile

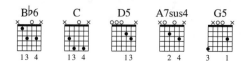

Bouzouki tuning:
(low to high) G-D-A-E

Gtr. 1: Drop D tuning:
(low to high) D-A-D-G-B-E

Intro
Moderately ♩ = 88

Verse

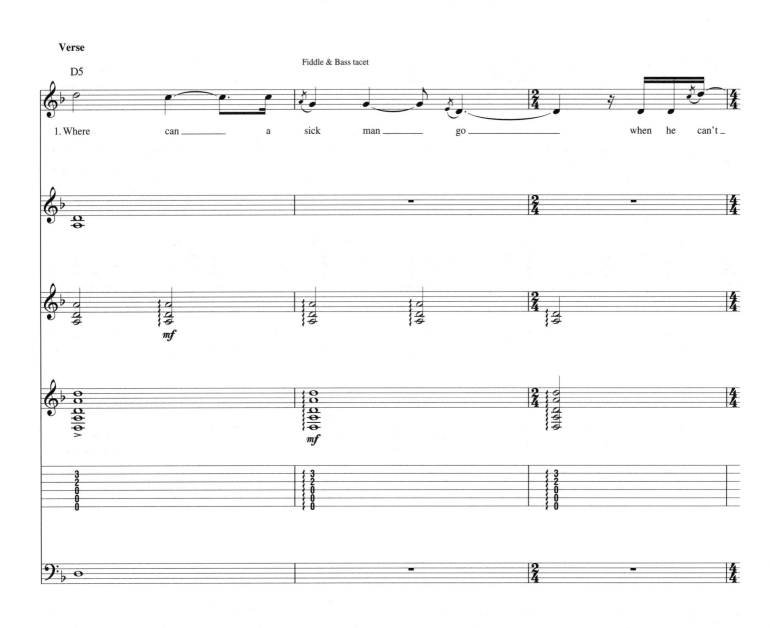

1. Where can a sick man go when he can't

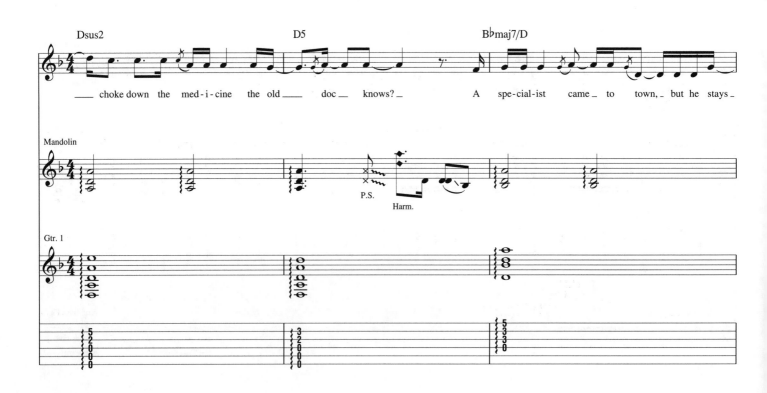

choke down the med-i-cine the old doc knows? A spe-cial-ist came to town, but he stays

at home, say-in' no one knows, so I don't, hon-ey, when in Rome.

Interlude

Mandolin: w/ Riff A
Gtr. 1: w/ Rhy. Fig. 1 (2 times)
Bass: w/ Bass Fig. 1 (1st 3 meas.)

Mandolin: w/ Riff B (1st meas.)

G5

Mandolin: w/ Riff B
Bass: w/ Bass Fig. 1 (last 3 meas.)

Gtr. 1: w/ Rhy. Fill 1

2. Where can _____ a teach - er _____ go? Wher-

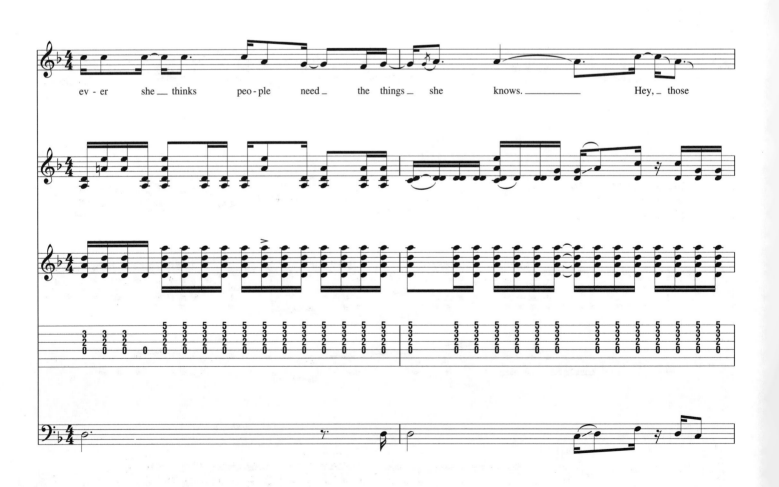

ev - er she _ thinks peo - ple need _ the things _ she knows. _____ Hey, _ those

*B♭maj7   B♭6

books you gave us look good on the shelves at home, and they'll burn

*Chord symbols reflect overall harmony.

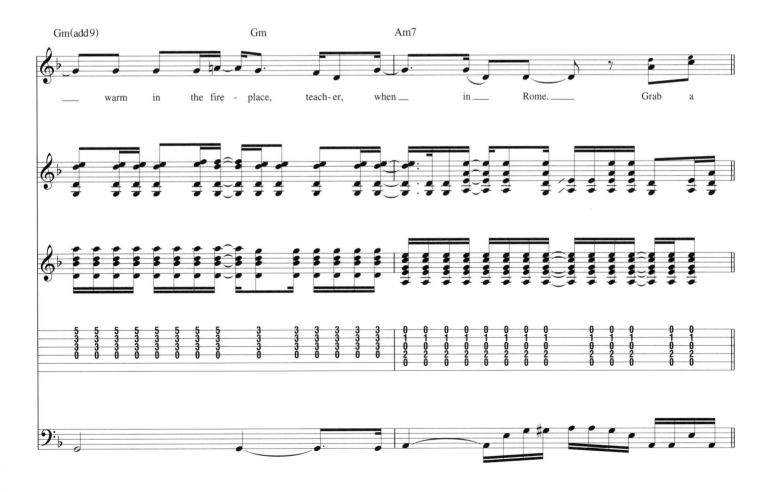

Gm(add9)   Gm   Am7

warm in the fire - place, teach-er, when in Rome. Grab a

Bridge

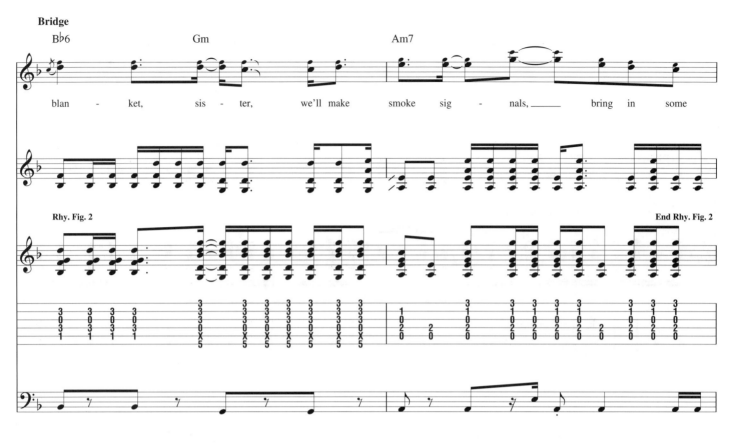

blan - ket, sis - ter, we'll make smoke sig - nals, _____ bring in some

Rhy. Fig. 2

End Rhy. Fig. 2

Gtr. 1: w/ Rhy. Fig. 2 (2 times)

new blood. _ It feels _ like we're a - lone. _____ Grab a

Mandolin

Bass

blan - ket, broth - er, so we don't catch _ cold _____ from one an -

oth - er.___ I won - der if we're stuck in ___

Interlude

Gtr. 1: w/ Rhy. Fig. 1 (1 3/4 times)
Bass: w/ Bass Fig. 1 (1st 3 meas.)

Rome.___

Fiddle

Mandolin

Bouzouki

Bass

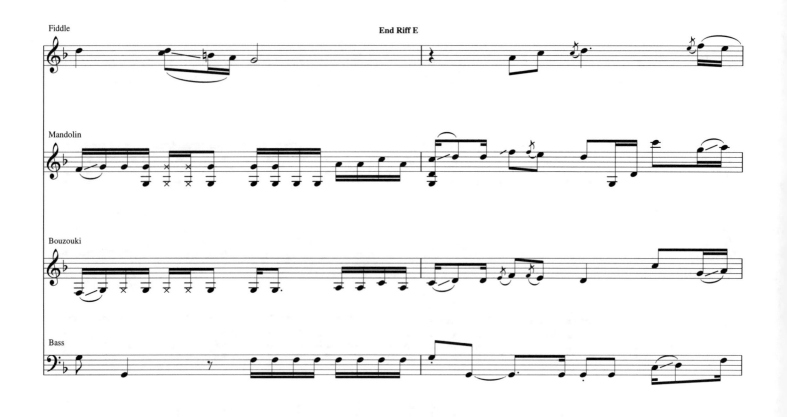

Verse
Bouzouki tacet   Bass tacet

3. Where can _____ a dead man _____ go? A ques -

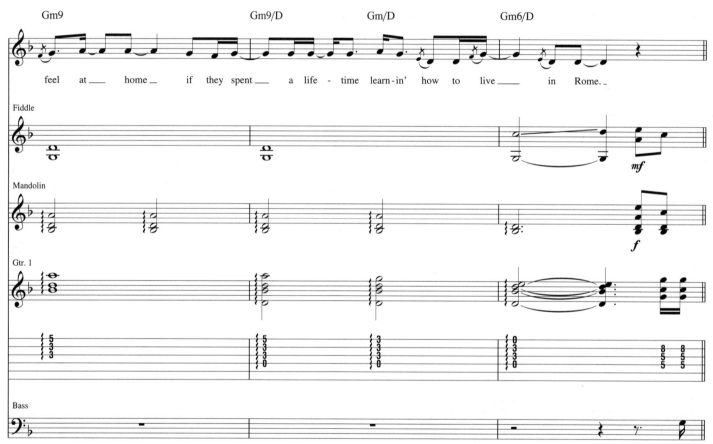

Outro

Fiddle: w/ Riff C (2 times)
Gtr. 1: w/ Rhy. Fig. 1 (2 times)
Bass: w/ Bass Fig. 1 (1st 2 meas.)

G5

Somebody More Like You

Words and Music by Sean Watkins

Gtrs. 1 & 2: Open G tuning, Capo II:
(low to high) D-G-D-G-B-D

Mandolas 1 & 2: Tuning:
(low to high) D#-F#-C#-G#

Intro

Moderately fast ♩ = 142

*Symbols in parentheses represent chord names respective to capoed guitar.
Symbols above represent actual sounding chords. Capoed fret is "0" in tab.
Chord symbols reflect implied harmony.

Verse

Gtrs. 1 & 2: w/ Riff A
Mandola 1 tacet

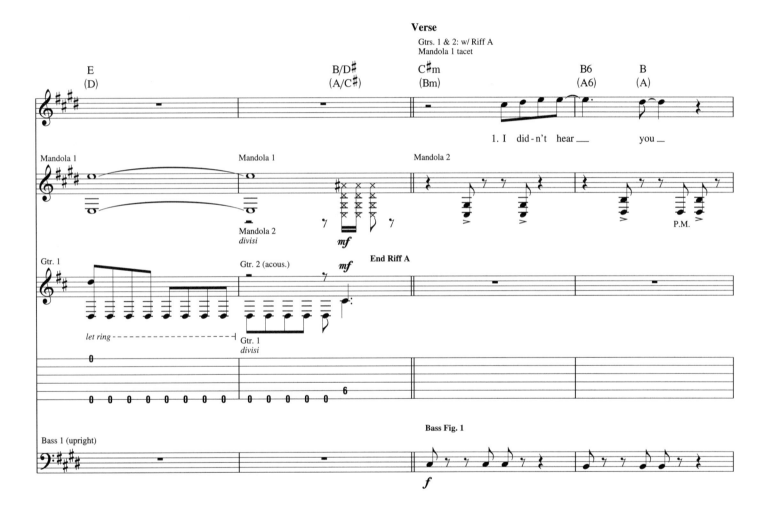

1. I did-n't hear ___ you ___

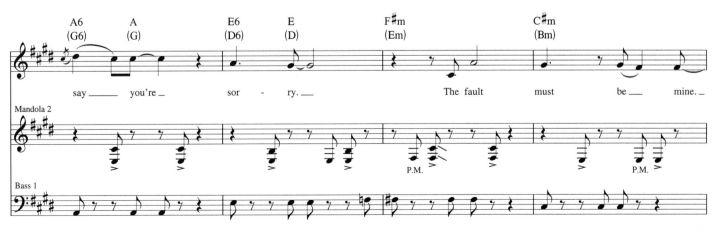

say ___ you're ___ sor - ry. ___ The fault must be ___ mine. ___

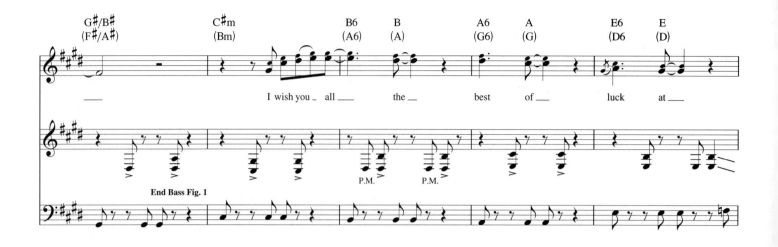

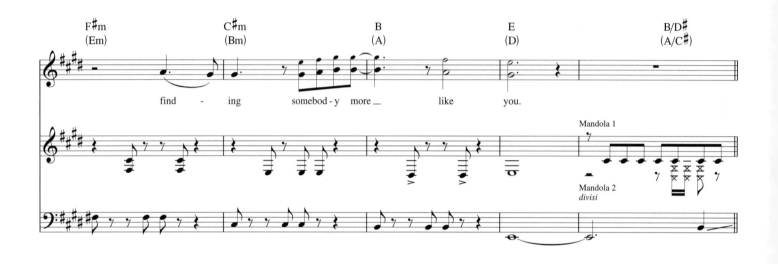

Verse

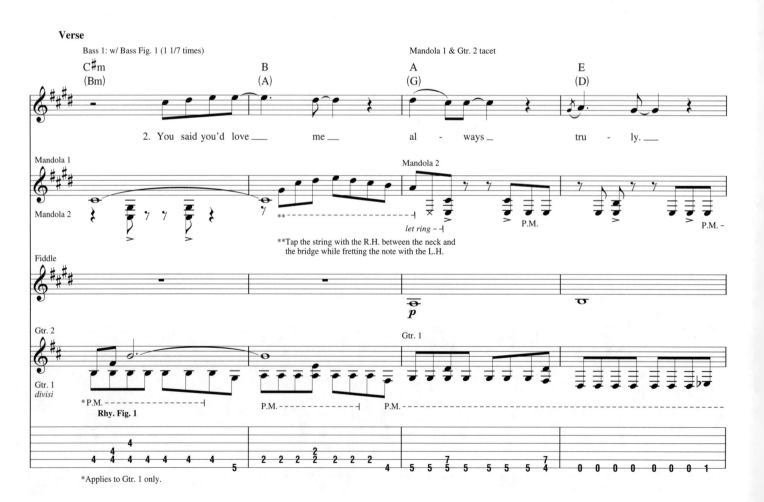

*Applies to Gtr. 1 only.

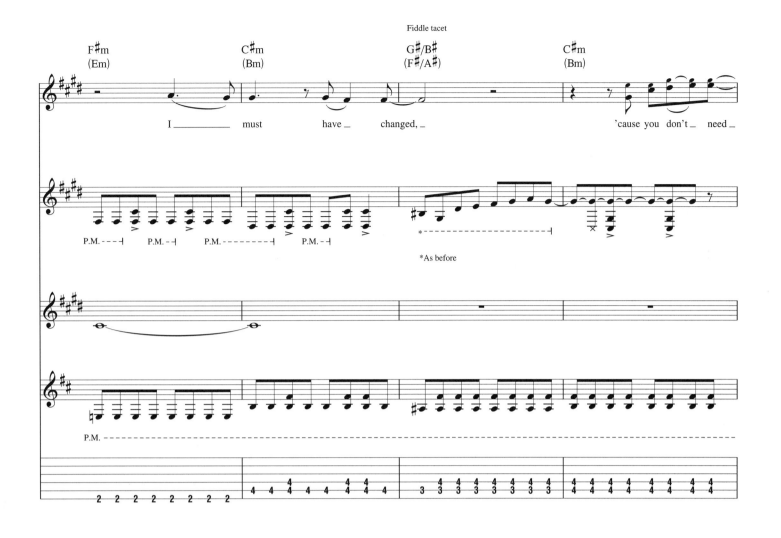

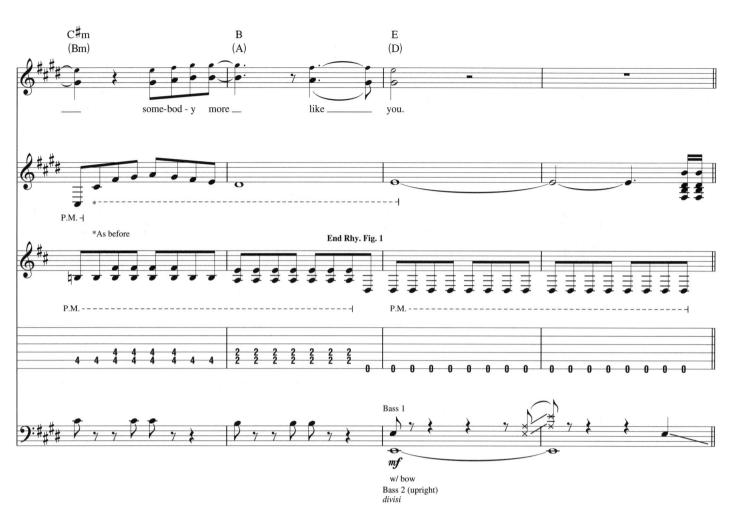

some-bod - y more ___ like ___ you.

*As before

End Rhy. Fig. 1

P.M.

Chorus

I hope you'll fi - n'ly find ___ some - one, ___ some-one that ___ you trust ___

(Ah.

Mandola 2

Mandola 1

Gtr. 1

Bass 1

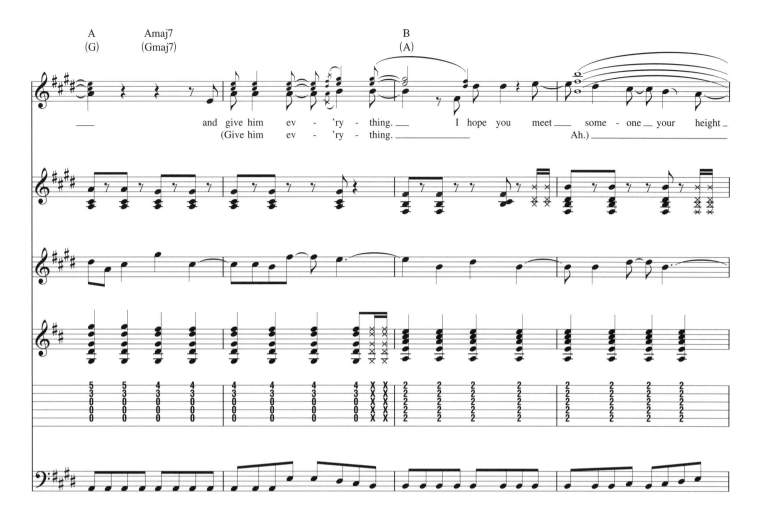

and give him ev - 'ry - thing. ___ I hope you meet ___ some - one ___ your ___ height ___
(Give him ev - 'ry - thing. _____ Ah.) _____

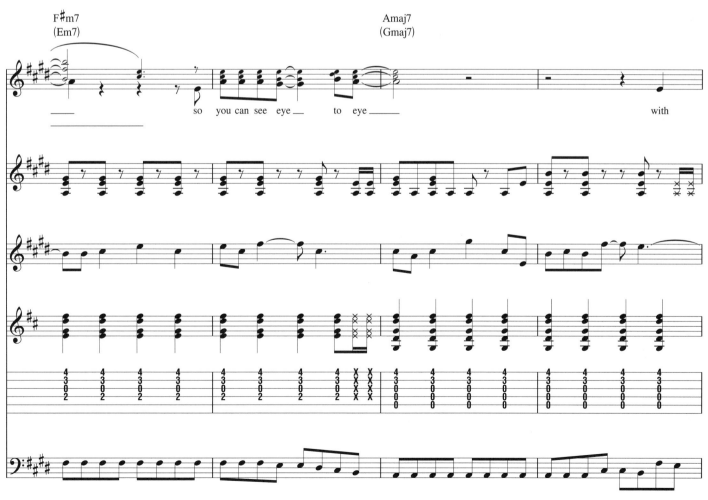

so you can see eye ___ to eye _____ with

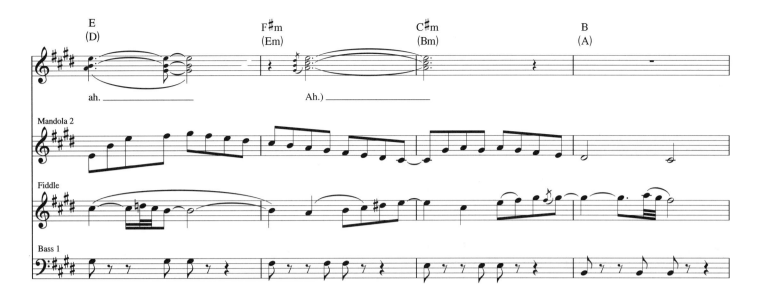

Fiddle tacet

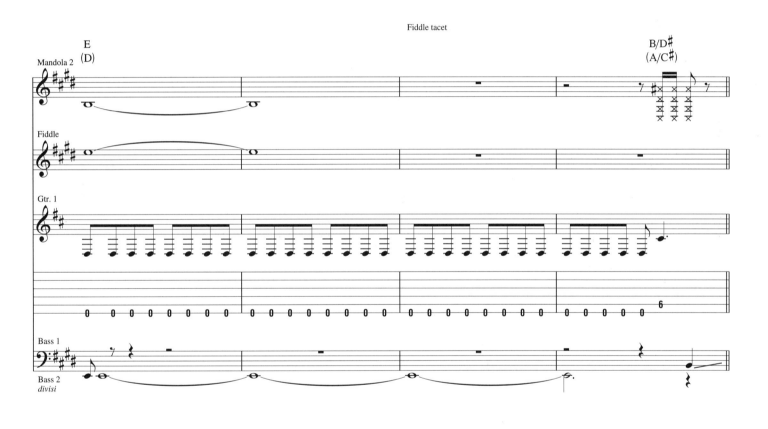

Verse

Gtr. 1: w/ Riff A (1st 12 meas.)
Bass 2 tacet

3. You came out of no - where, _____ and made _____ me _____

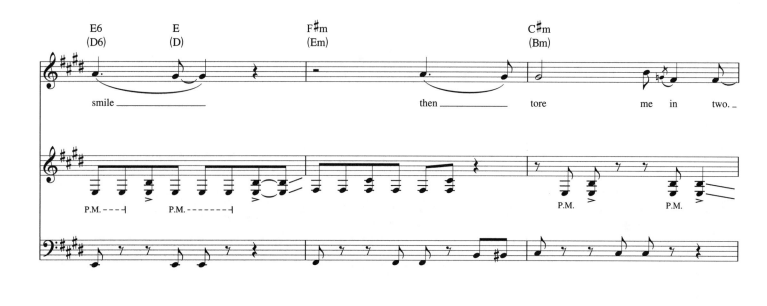

24

Jealous of the Moon

Words and Music by Chris Thile and Gary Louris

but you have-n't worn the old one yet. You've come too

far

to turn a - round

now. You're giv-in' up the good fight

when you're as strong _____ as an-y-one. _____ You're back where you _____

_____ start - ed from. _____ I see you're _____ back where _____ you

_____ start - ed from. _____

can do   if you're too   scared ___ to   try.

Interlude

Verse

31

Chorus

Star - in' down ___ the stars, ___ jeal - ous of ___ the moon. ___

You wish you ___ could fly. ___

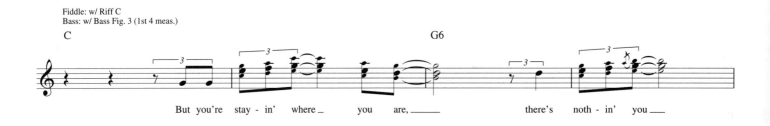

But you're stay - in' where ___ you are, ___ there's noth - in' you ___

can do ___ if you're too scared ___ to try.

Verse

Mandolin: w/ Riff B
Bass tacet

Chorus

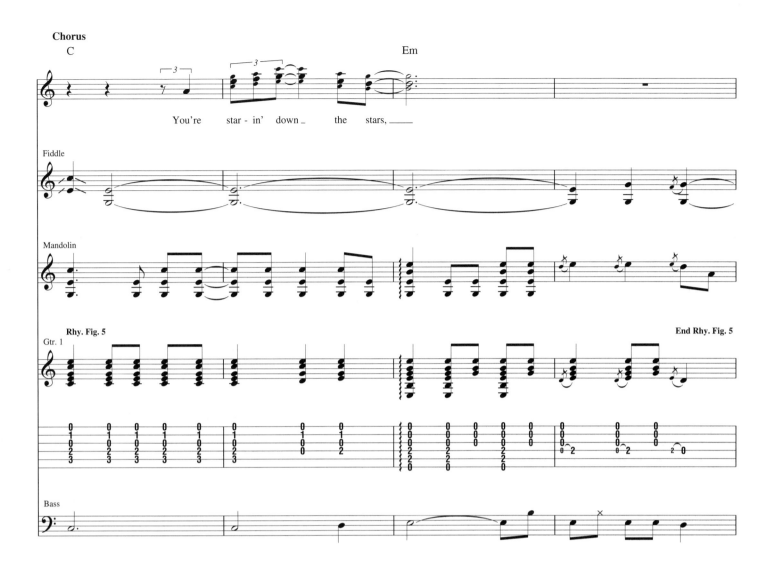

You're star - in' down the stars,

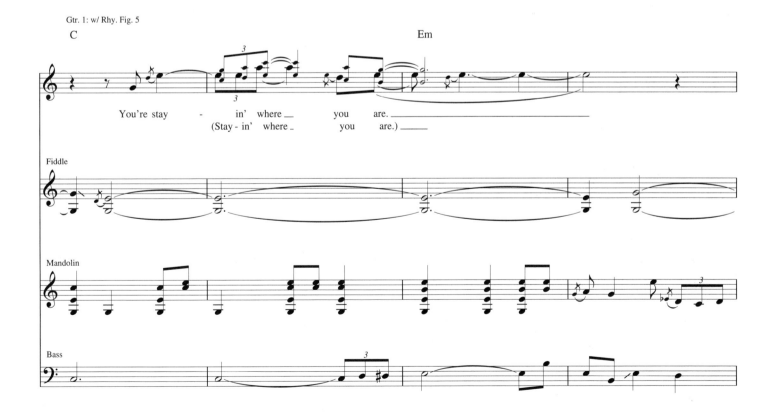

You're stay - in' where you are.
(Stay - in' where you are.)

if you're too _____ scared _____ to try.

Outro

Mandolin & Gtr. 1: w/ Riffs A & A1

Scotch and Chocolate

By Chris Thile, Sean Watkins and Sara Watkins

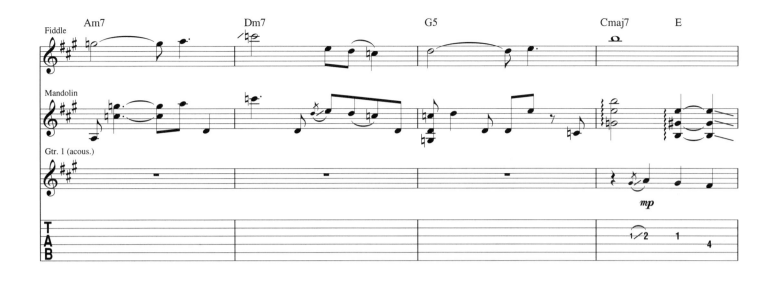

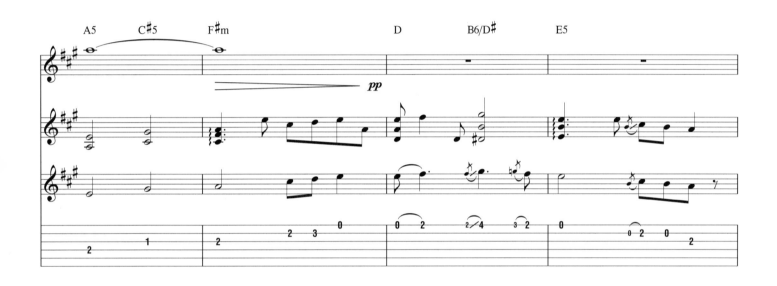

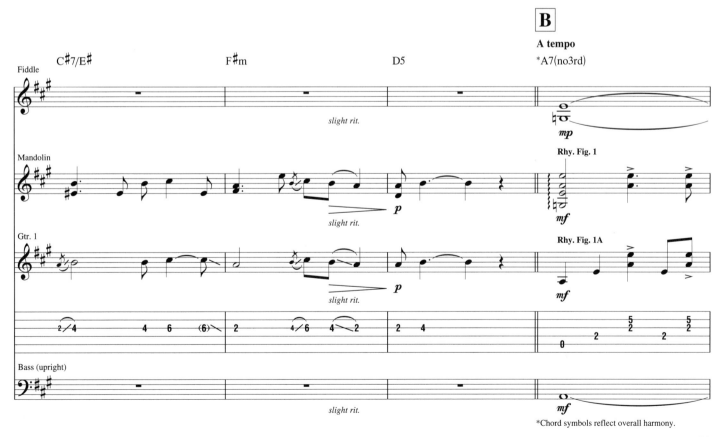

*Chord symbols reflect overall harmony.

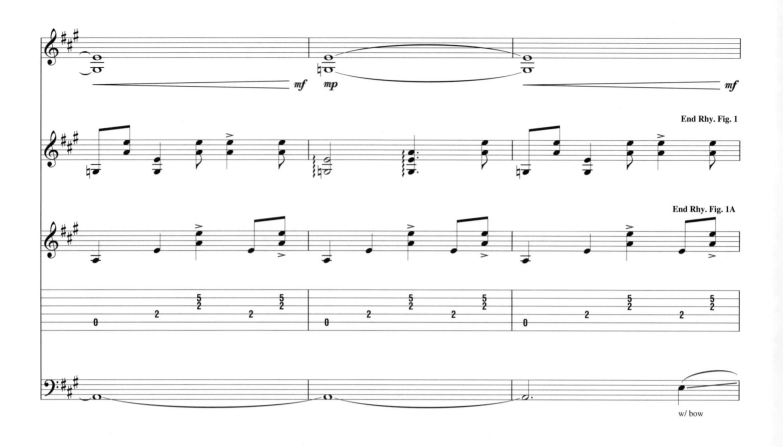

End Rhy. Fig. 1

End Rhy. Fig. 1A

w/ bow

Mandolin & Gtr. 1: w/ Rhy. Figs. 1 & 1A

A7

G5   F♯5   Em

End Riff A   **Riff B**

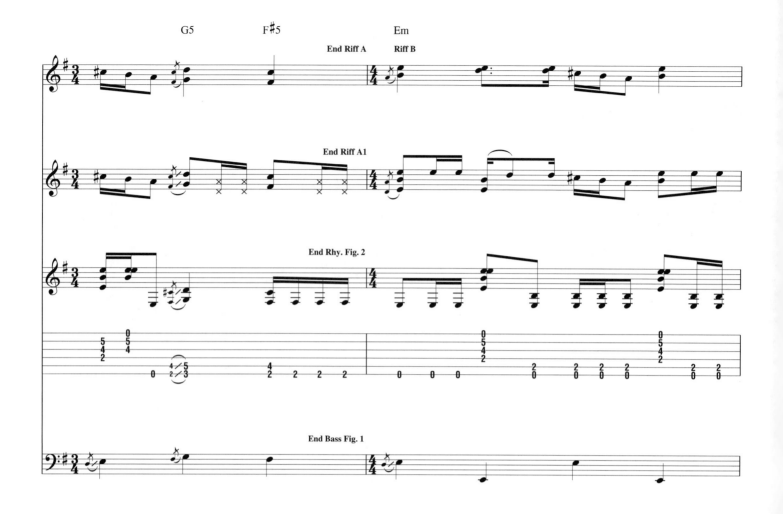

44

D

Asus2

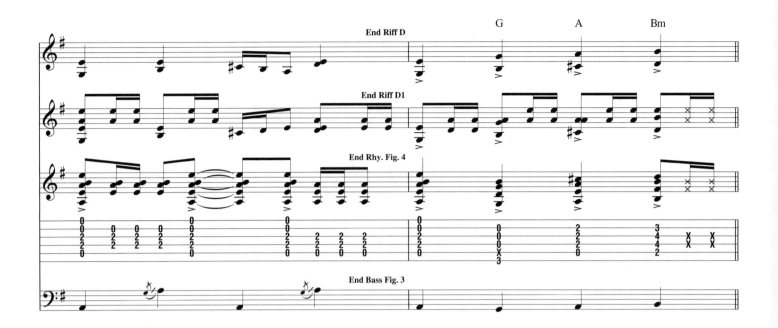

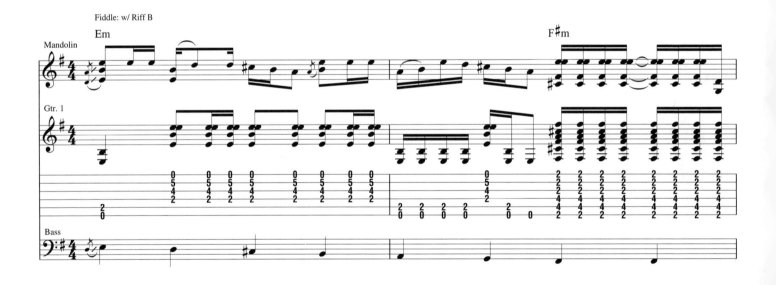

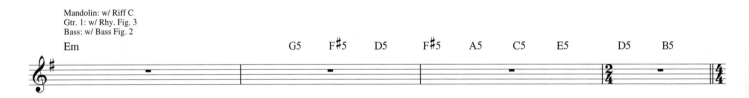

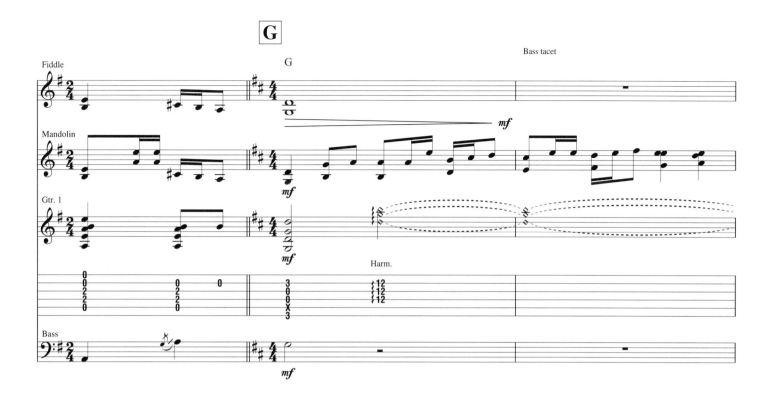

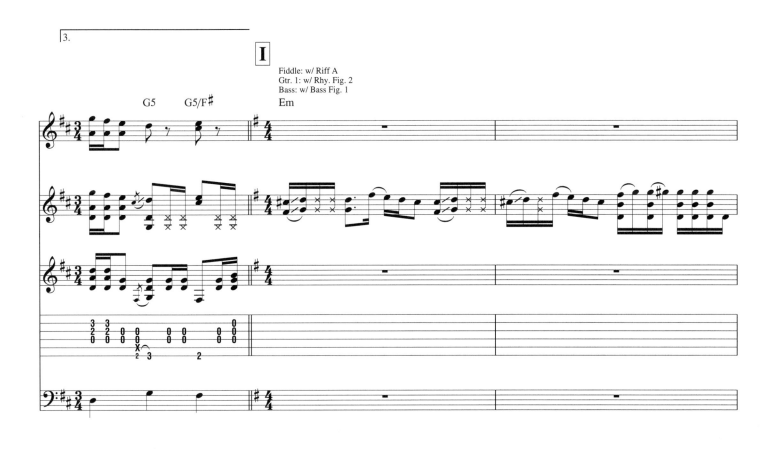

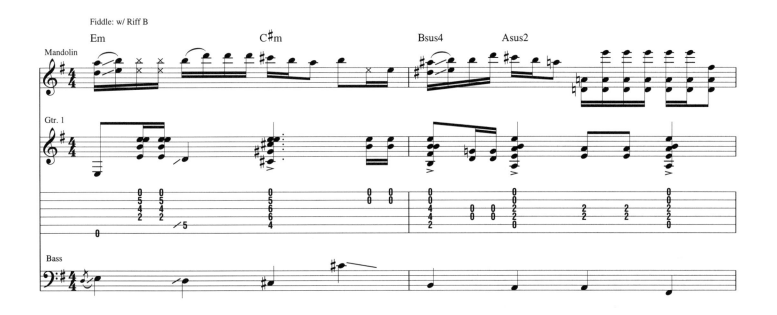

Can't Complain

Words and Music by Chris Thile

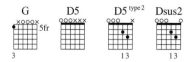

Gtr. 1 (Tenor gtr.) tuning:
(low to high) ↓G–↓D–↓A–↓E

Gtr. 2: Drop D tuning:
(low to high) D–A–D–G–B–E

Intro

Moderately slow ♩ = 79

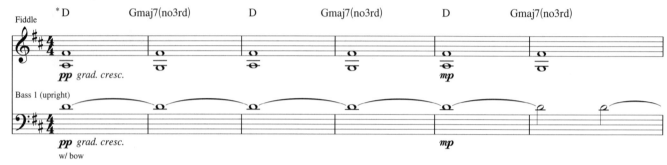

*Chord symbols reflect overall harmony.

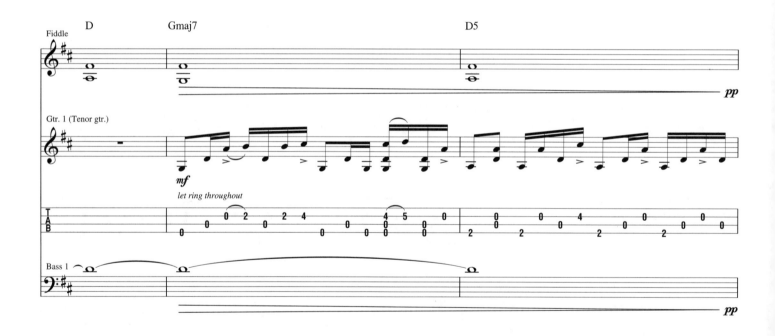

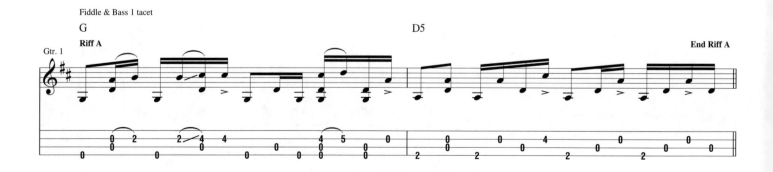

Verse

Gtr. 1: w/ Riff A (5 times)

G   D5   G

1. I made her smile, _ I made _ her cry. _   Cleared her head _ and made _ her won - der _ why. _

Gtr. 2 (nylon-str. acous.)

mp
w/ fingers
let ring throughout
Harm.

D5   G   D5

_ I helped her live _ and made _ her wan - na die, _   but she _

Riff B   End Riff B

mf

Gtr. 2: w/ Riff B (2 times)

G   D5   G   D5

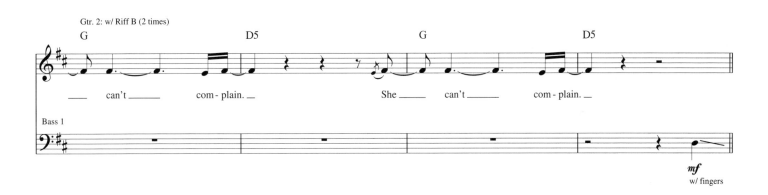

_ can't _ com - plain. _   She _ can't _ com - plain. _

Bass 1

mf
w/ fingers

Verse

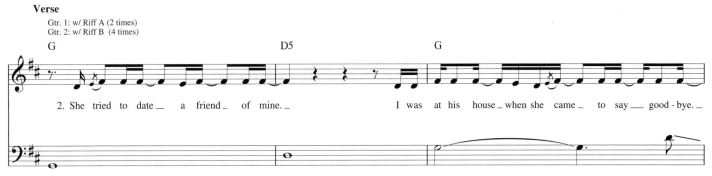

Gtr. 1: w/ Riff A (2 times)
Gtr. 2: w/ Riff B (4 times)

G   D5   G

2. She tried to date _ a friend _ of mine. _   I was at his house _ when she came _ to say _ good-bye. _

He __ stood her up, __ but she took it __ as __ a sign __ and I __

__ can't __ com - plain. __ I __

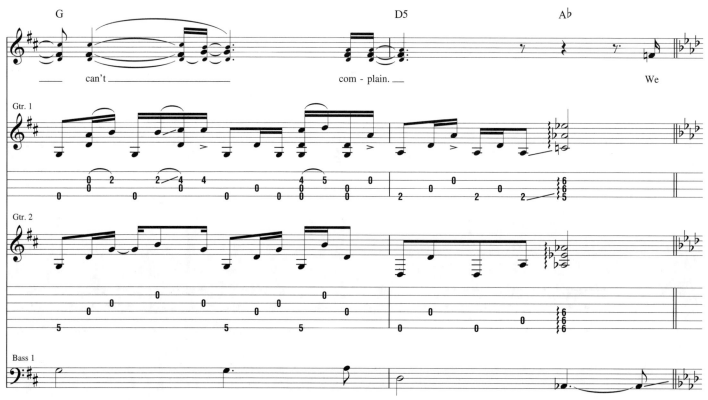

__ can't __ com - plain. __ We

Bridge

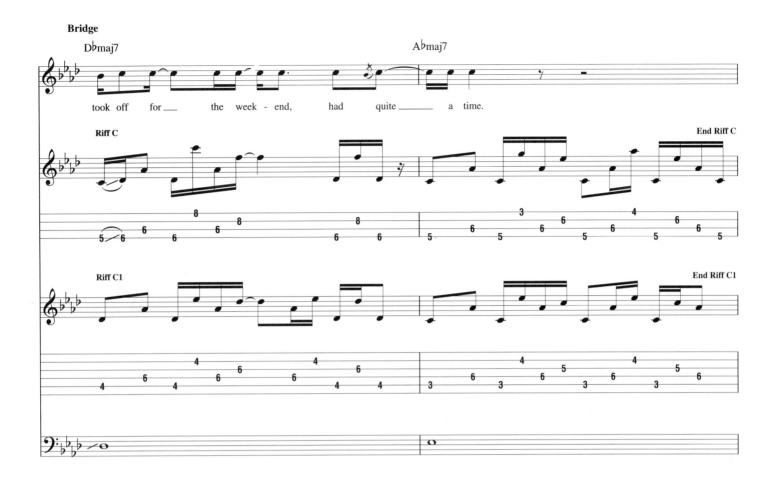

took off for ___ the week-end, had quite ___ a time.

Gtr. 1: w/ Riff C
Gtr. 2: w/ Riff C1 (3 1/2 times)

Shared ev - 'ry - thing ___ we'd ev - er tried. ___   I

told her I ___ could love ___ her, I told her I ___ could lie.   So she ___

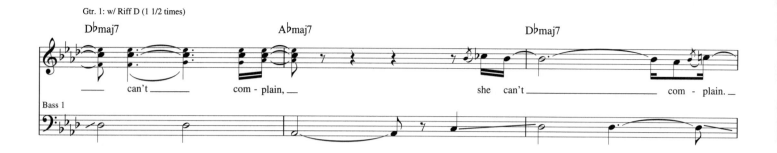

Verse

She couldn't see ___ the end, _ but nei - ther could I. ____ So I can't _

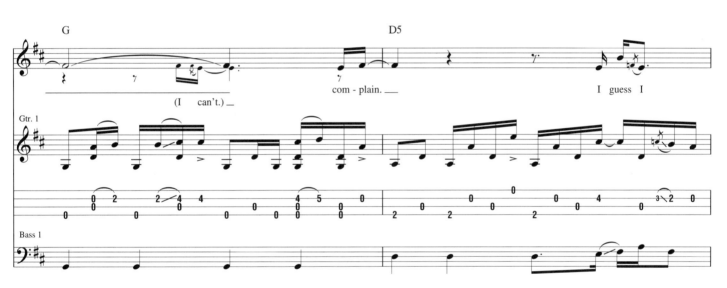

(I   can't.) _____   com - plain. ___   I   guess I

can't _____   com - plain. ___

Bridge

She moved here __ and bought the first house she could find. __ I __

Gtr. 1: w/ Rhy. Fig. 1
Gtr. 2: w/ Riff E (2 1/2 times)
Bass 1: w/ Bass Fig. 1 (2 1/2 times)
Bass 2 tacet

__ moved in __ and we locked __ our - selves __ in - side. __ I

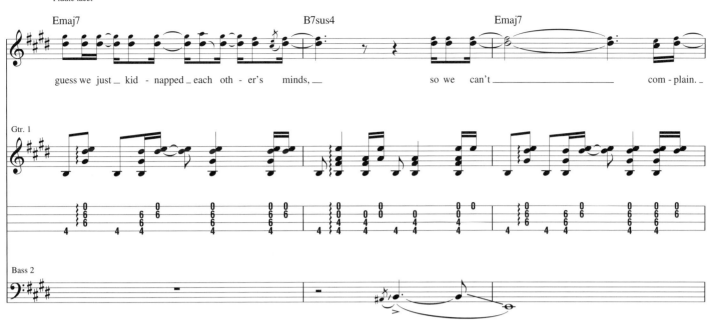

guess we just __ kid - napped __ each oth - er's minds, __ so we can't _____ com - plain. __

__ We __ can't _____ com - plain. __ Mm, __

(We can't _____ com - plain.) __

(We can't _____ com - plain.) __

Interlude

Gtr. 2: w/ Riff E

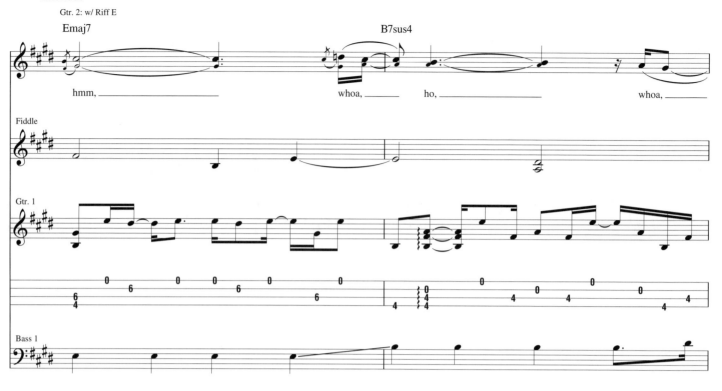

hmm, _____ whoa, _____ ho, _____ whoa, _____

___ mm, _____ hmm. 4. I

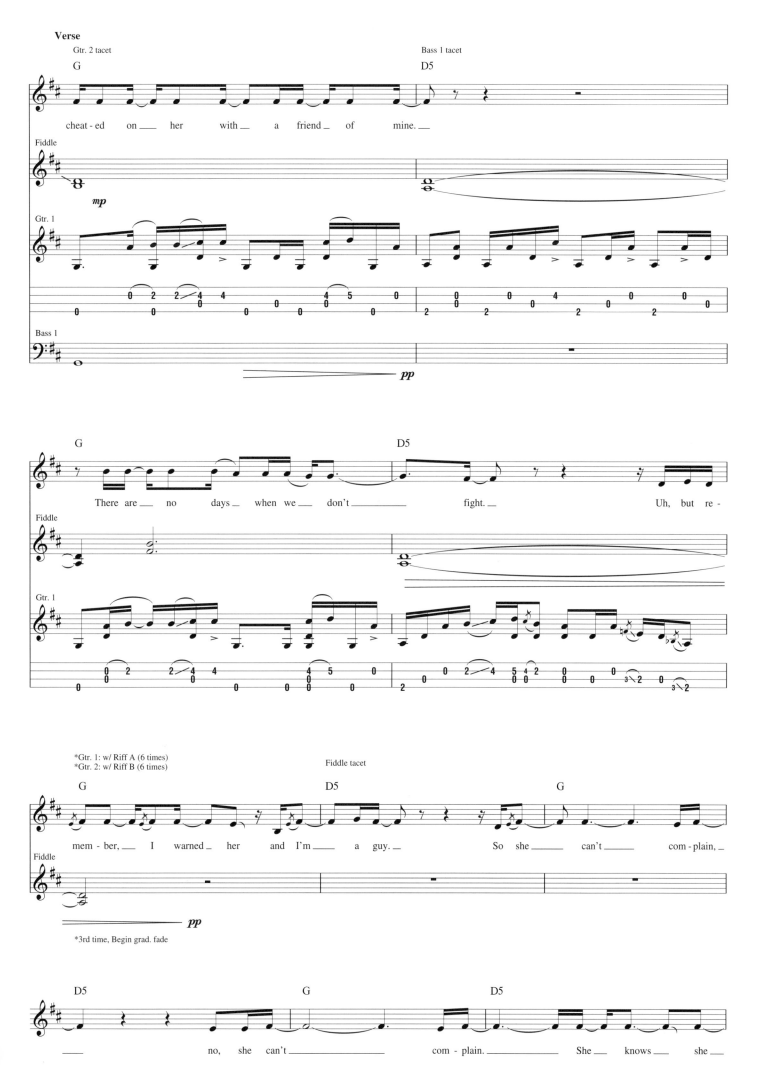

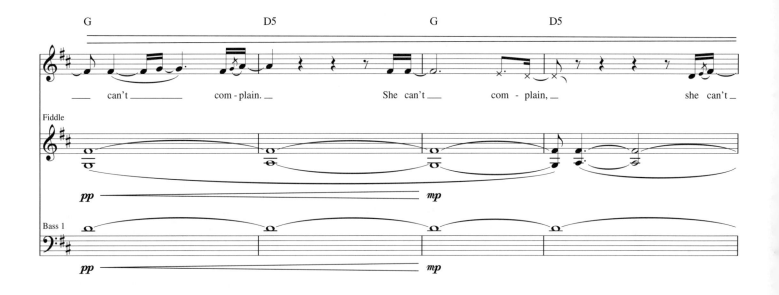

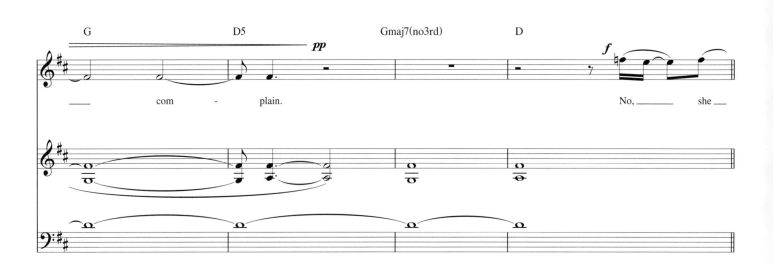

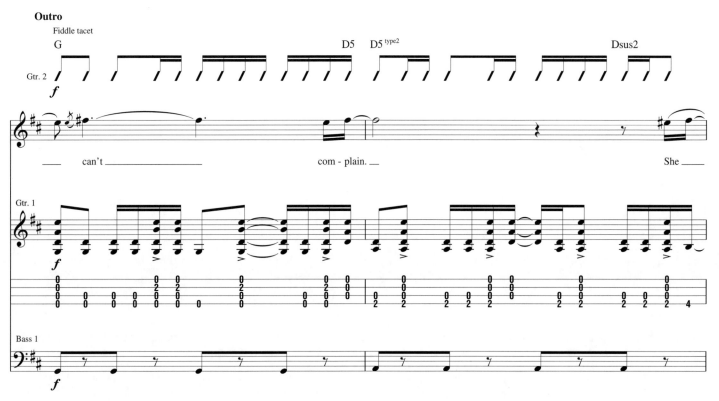

*Refers to downstemmed voc. only.

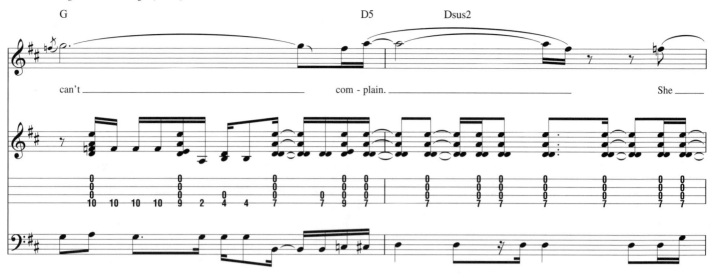

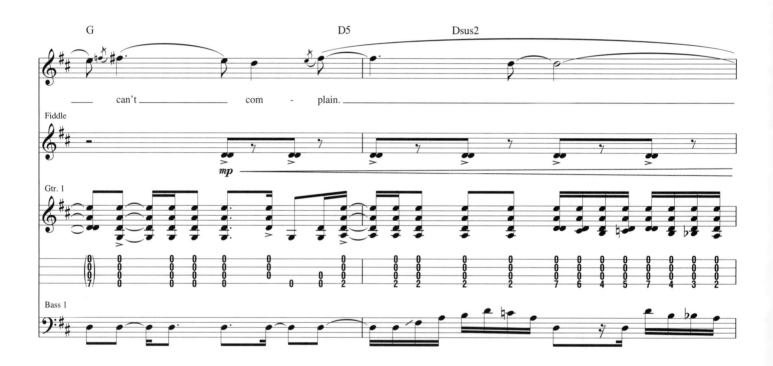

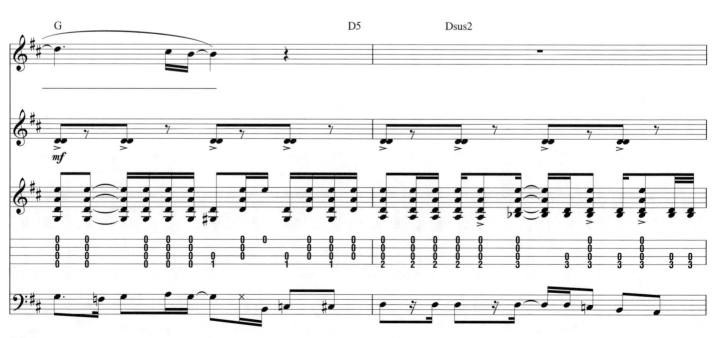

Tomorrow Is a Long Time

Words and Music by Bob Dylan

Gtr. 1: Capo I

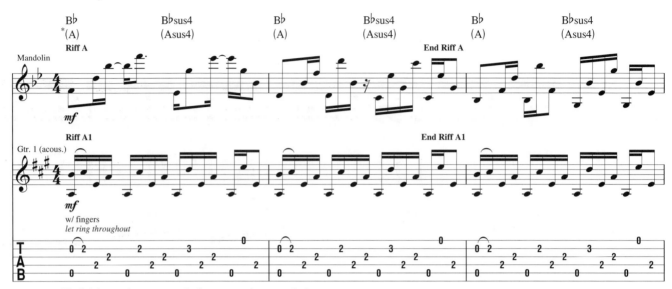

*Symbols in parentheses represent chord names respective to capoed guitar.
Symbols above reflect actual sounding chords. Capoed fret is "0" in tab.

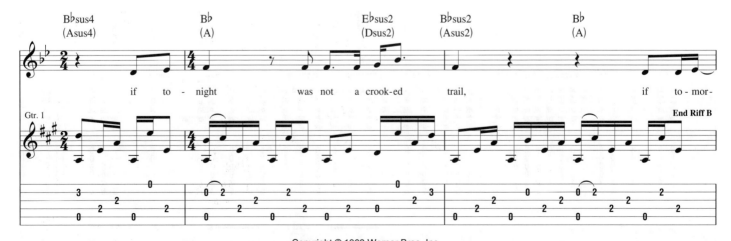

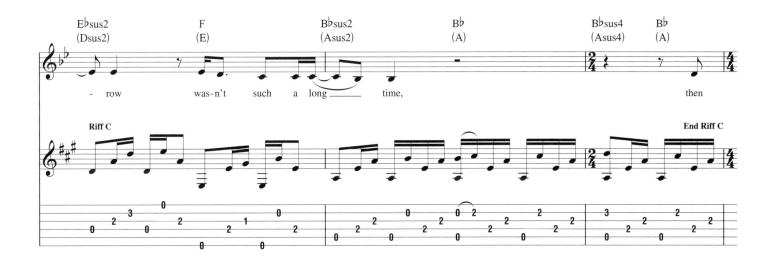

Chorus

Gtr. 1: w/ Riff E

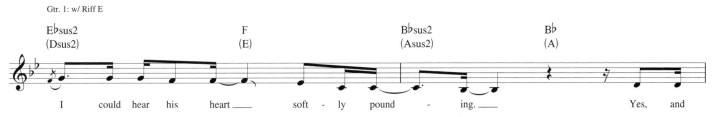

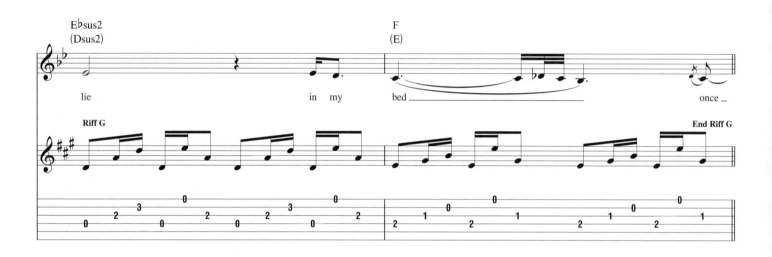

Interlude

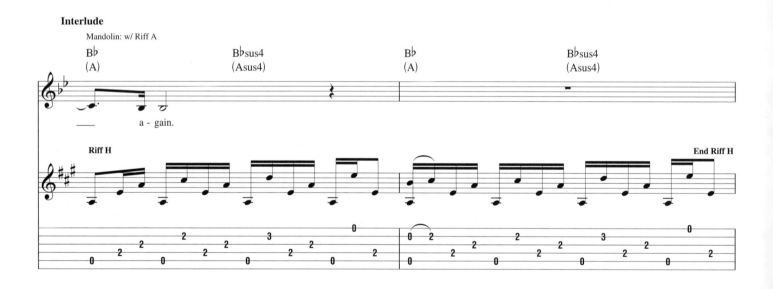

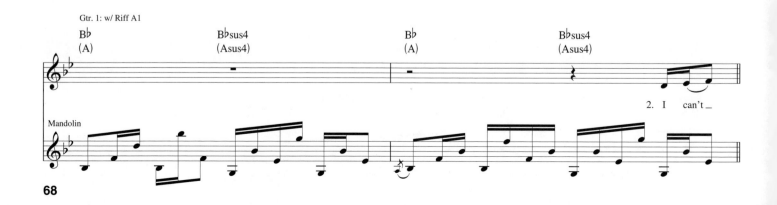

Chorus

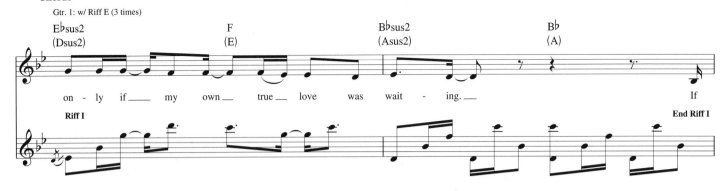

on - ly if my own true love was wait - ing. If

Mandolin: w/ Riff I (1 1/2 times)

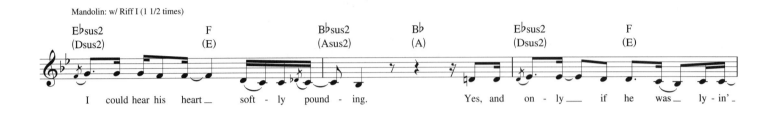

I could hear his heart soft - ly pound - ing. Yes, and on - ly if he was ly - in'

by me would I lie in my bed once

Interlude

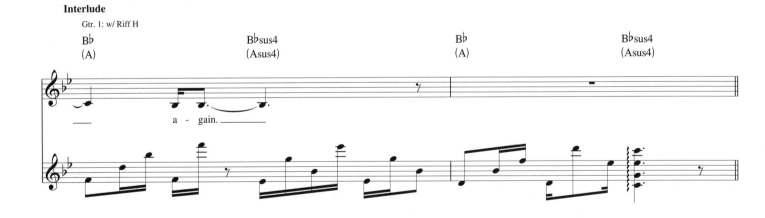

a - gain.

Fiddle/Mandolin Solo

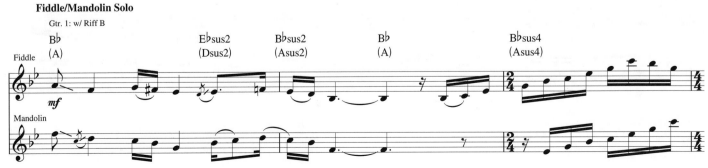

Verse

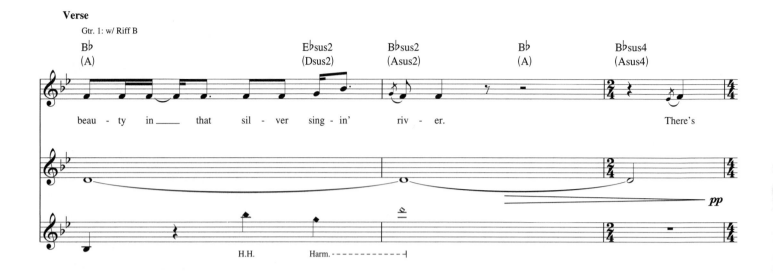

Gtr. 1: w/ Riff B

beau - ty in ____ that sil - ver sing - in' riv - er. There's

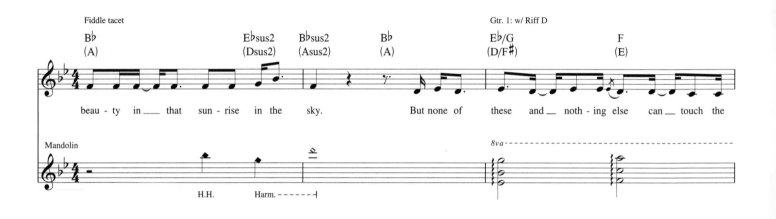

Fiddle tacet · Gtr. 1: w/ Riff D

beau - ty in ____ that sun - rise in the sky. But none of these and ____ noth - ing else can ____ touch the

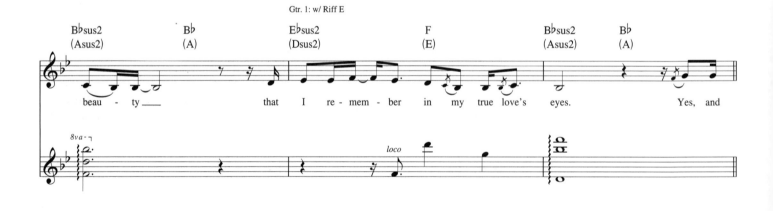

Gtr. 1: w/ Riff E

beau - ty ____ that I re - mem - ber in my true love's eyes. Yes, and

Chorus

Gtr. 1: w/ Riff E (2 times)

on - ly if ____ my own ____ true ____ love was wait - ing. ____ If

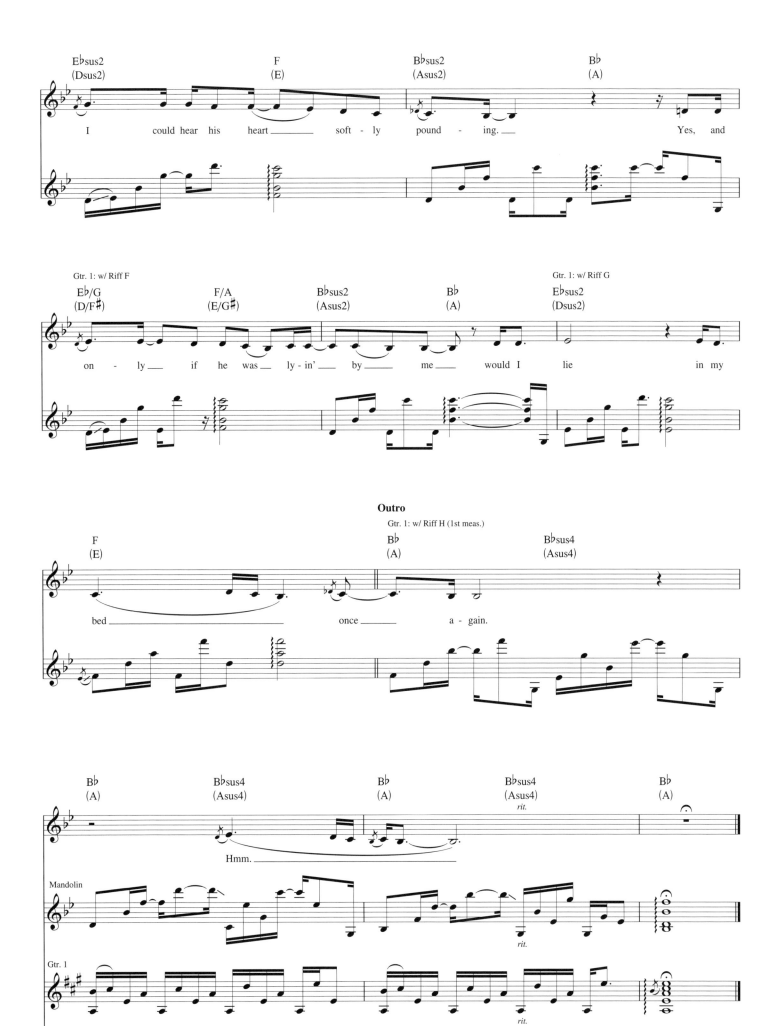

Eveline

Words and Music by Chris Thile and Sean Watkins

Gtr. 1: Tune down 2 steps:
(low to high) C-F-B♭-E♭-G-C

Bass tuning:
(low to high) C-A-D-G

*Symbols in parentheses represent chord names respective to detuned guitar.
Symbols above reflect actual sounding chords.
Chord symbols reflect overall harmony.

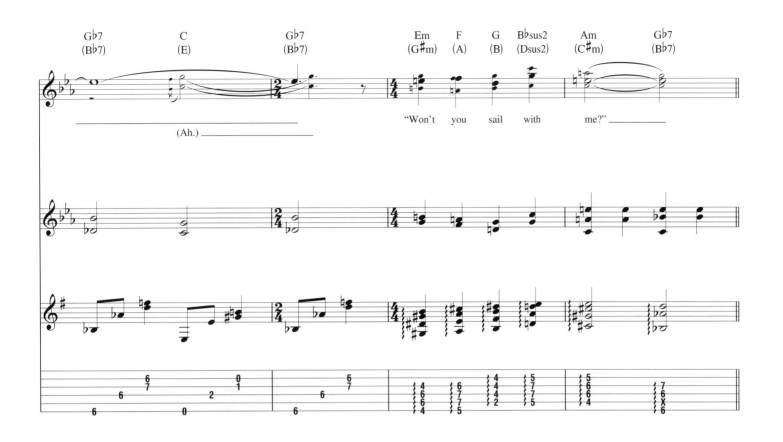

"Won't you sail with me?"

(Ah.)

Interlude

Verse

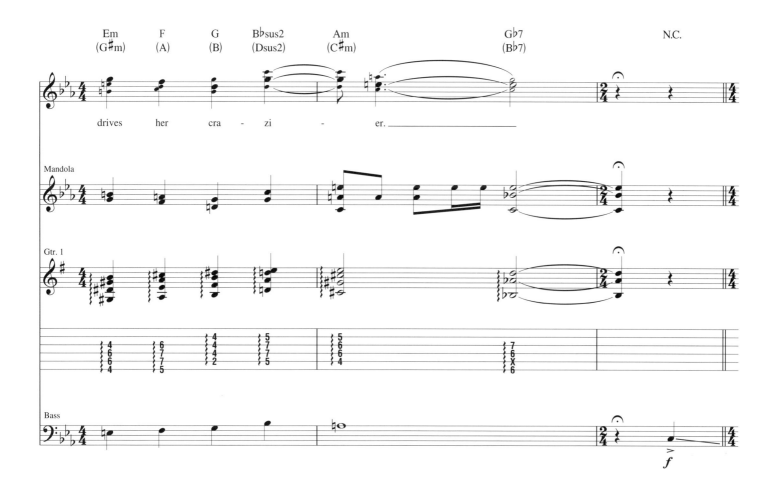

Interlude

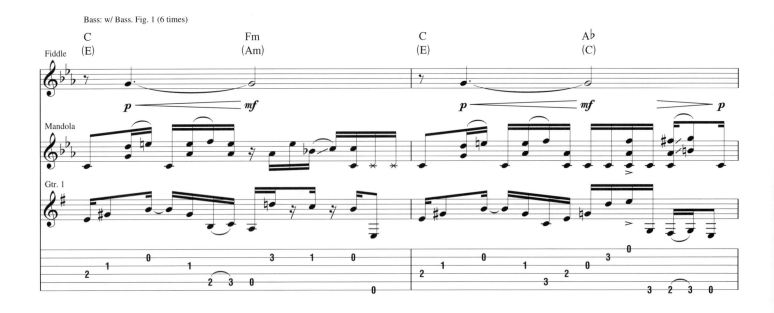

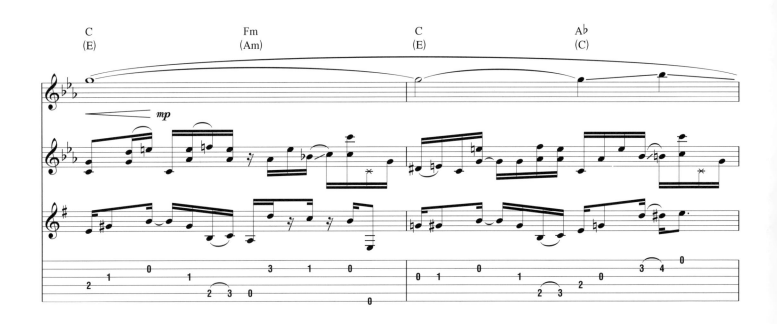

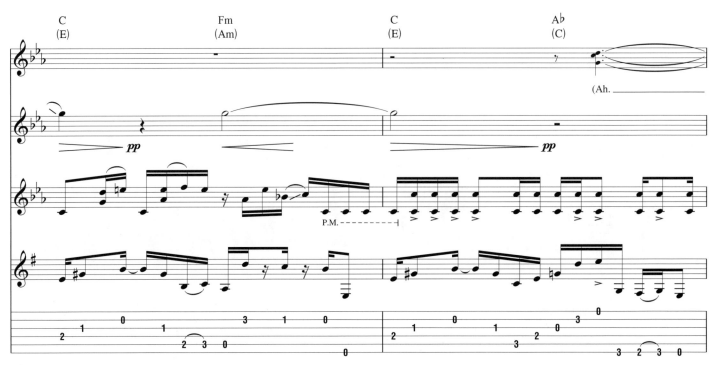

Verse

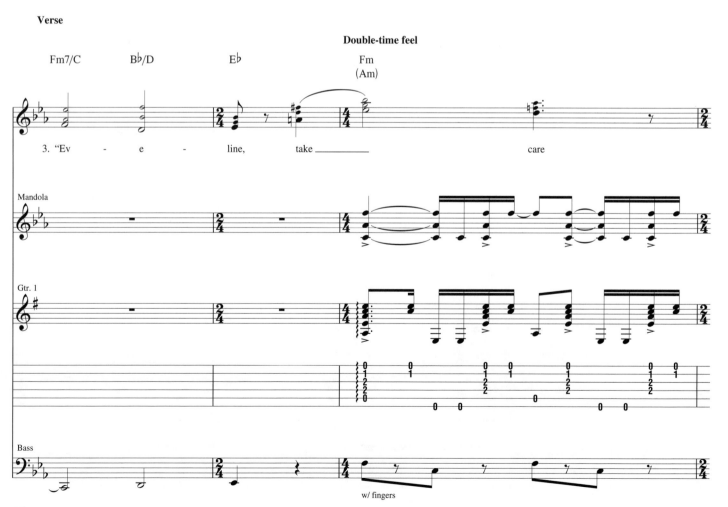

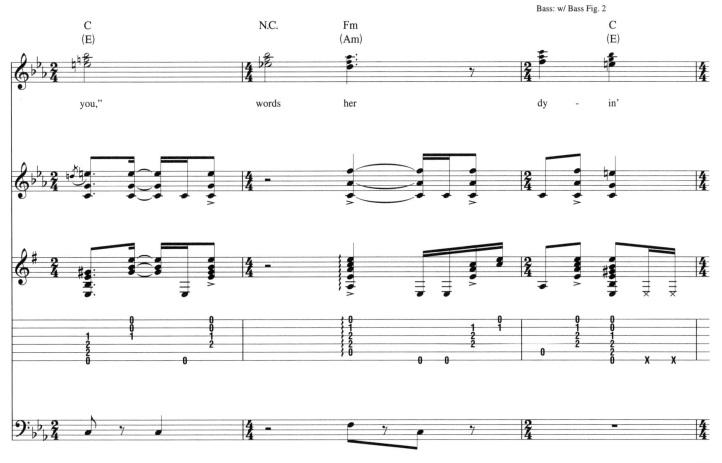

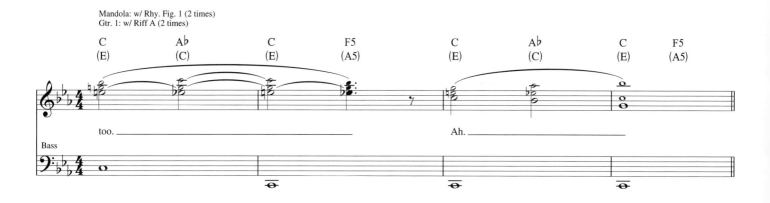

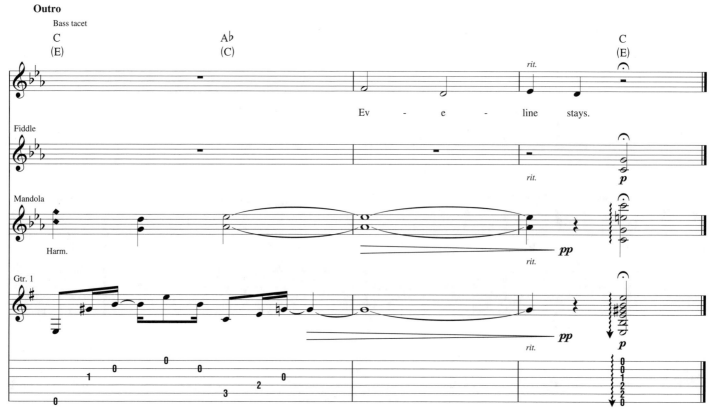

Stumptown

By Chris Thile

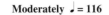

*Symbols in parentheses represent chord names respective to capoed guitar.
Symbols above represent actual sounding chords. Capoed fret is "0" in tab.
Chord symbols reflect overall harmony.

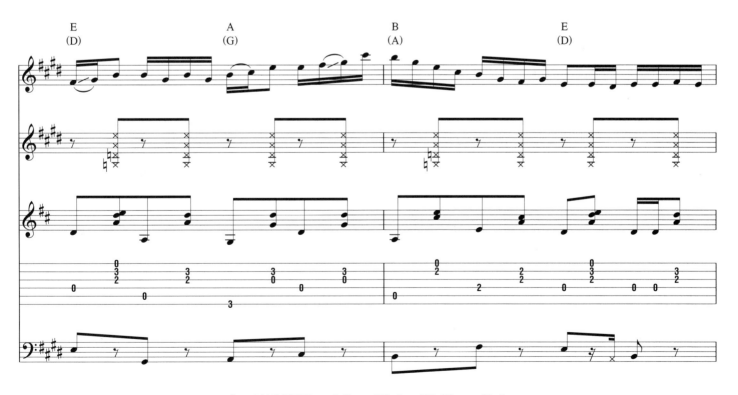

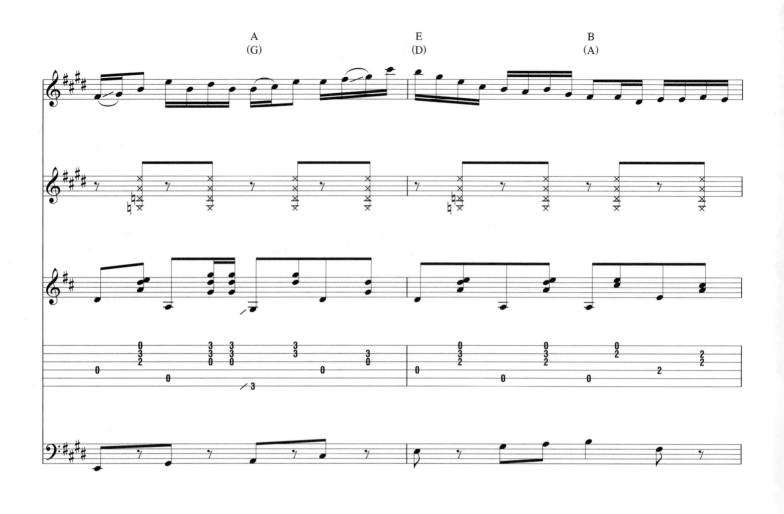

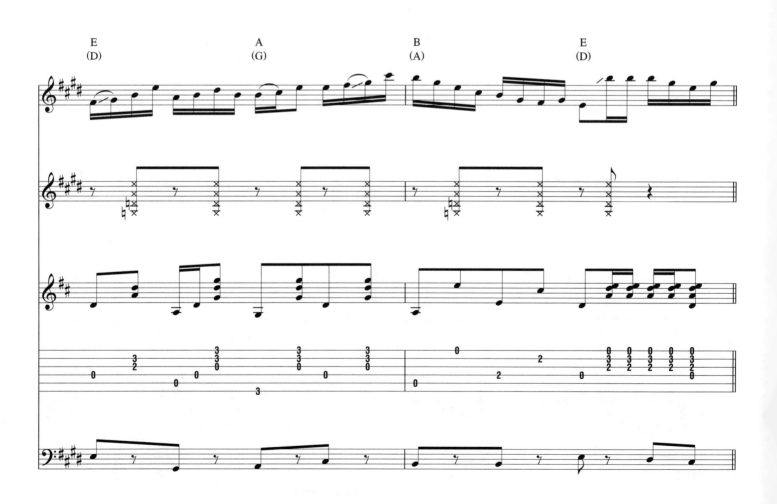

B

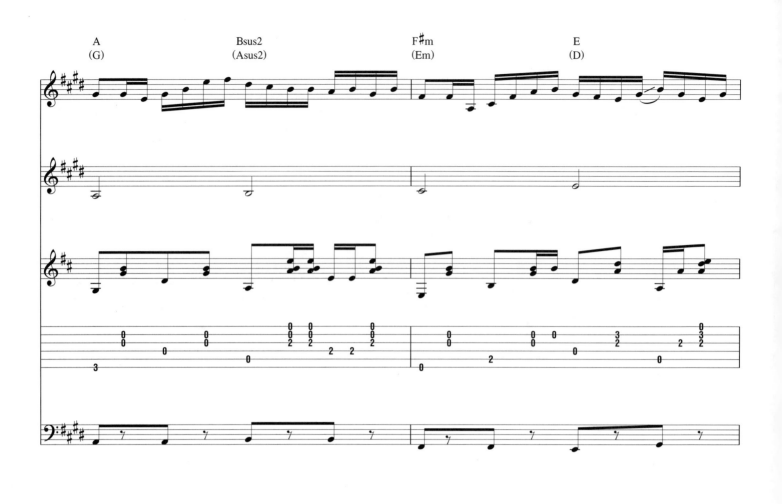

C

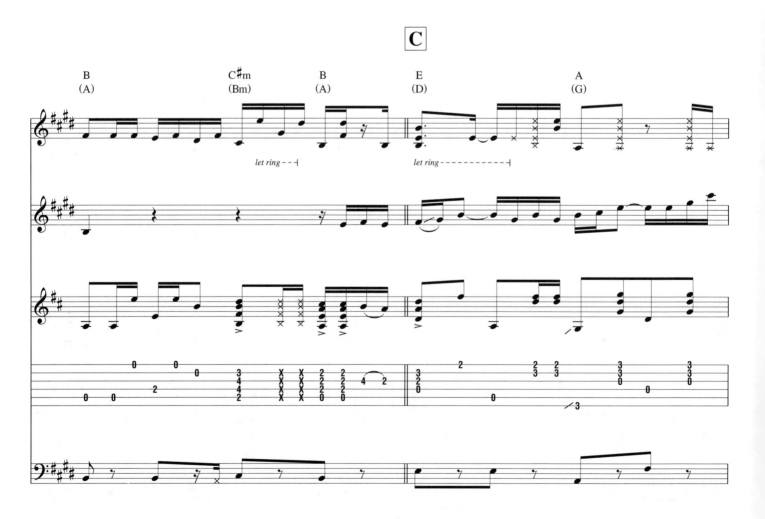

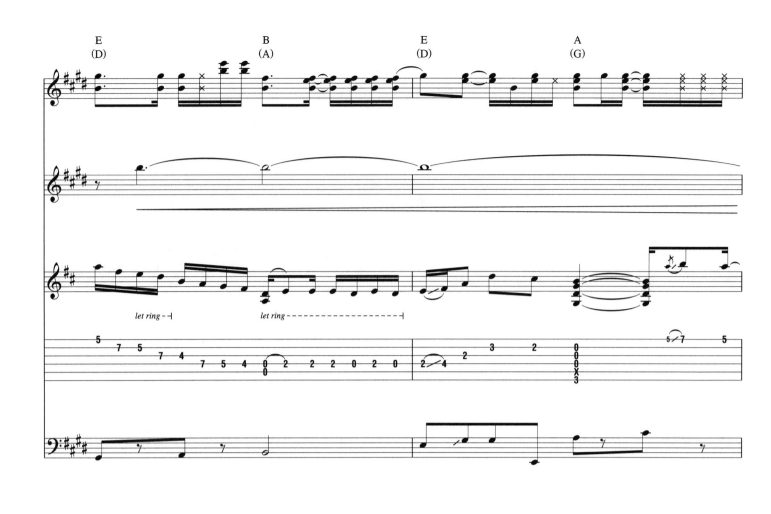

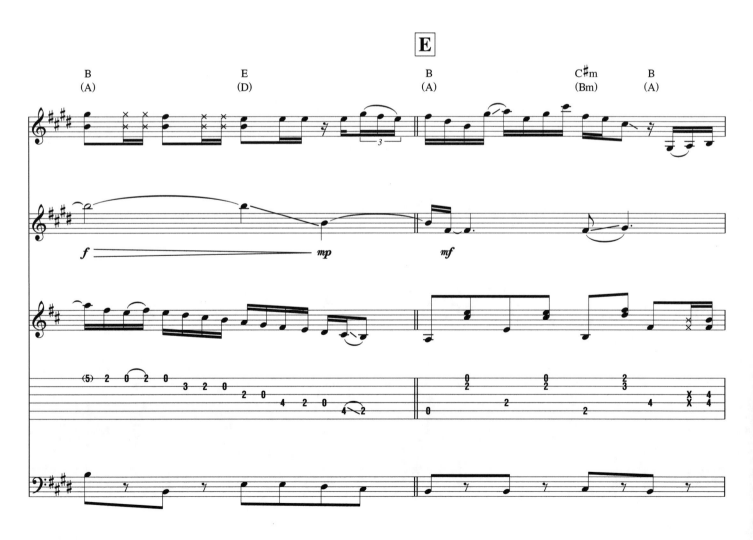

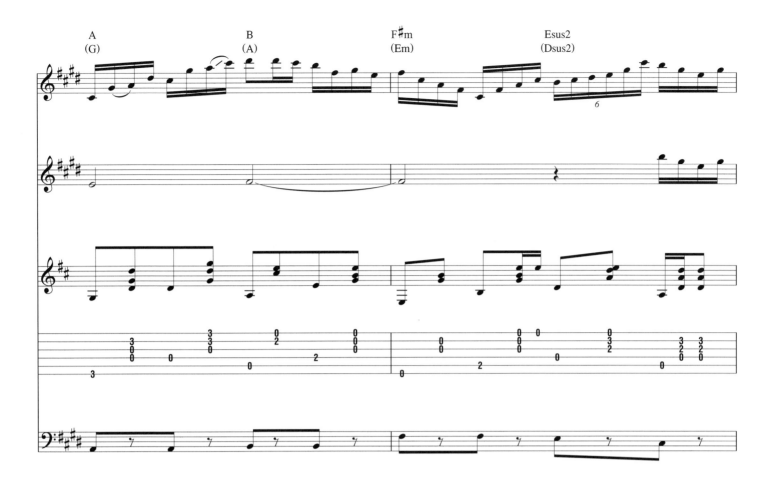

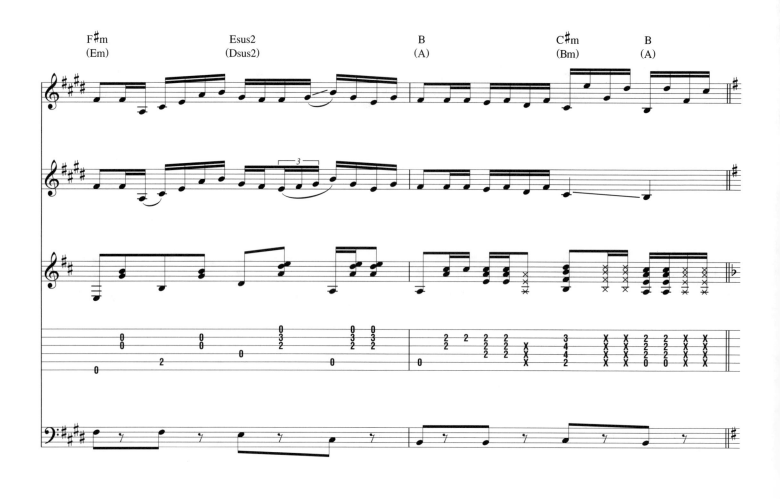

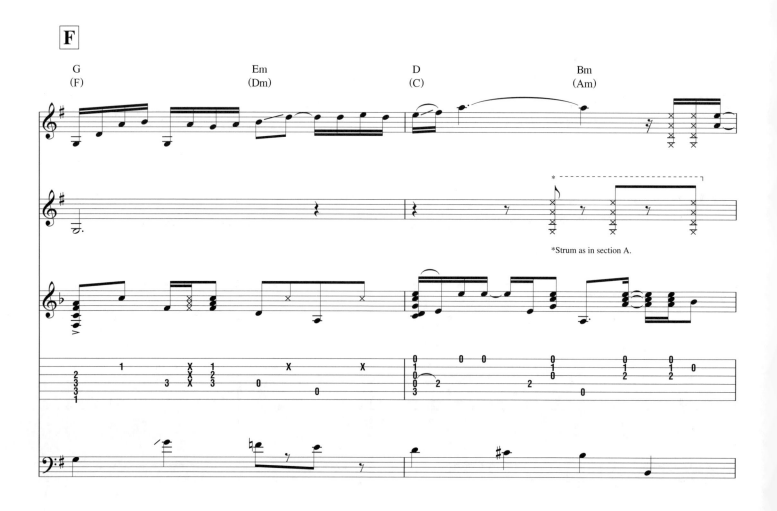

*Strum as in section A.

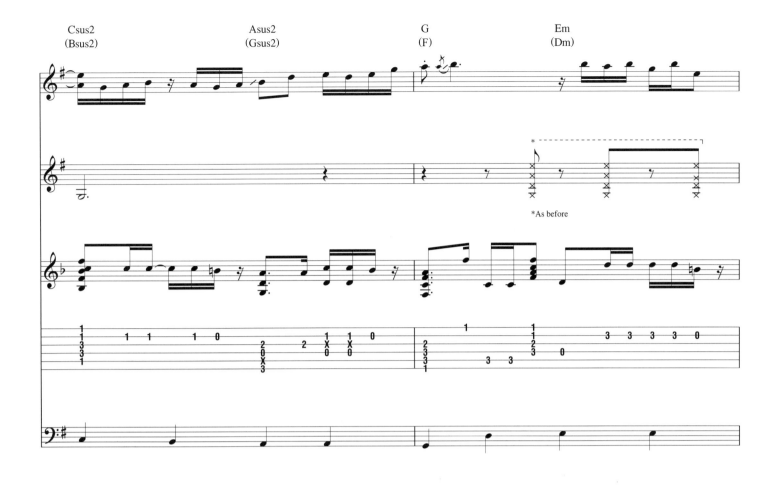

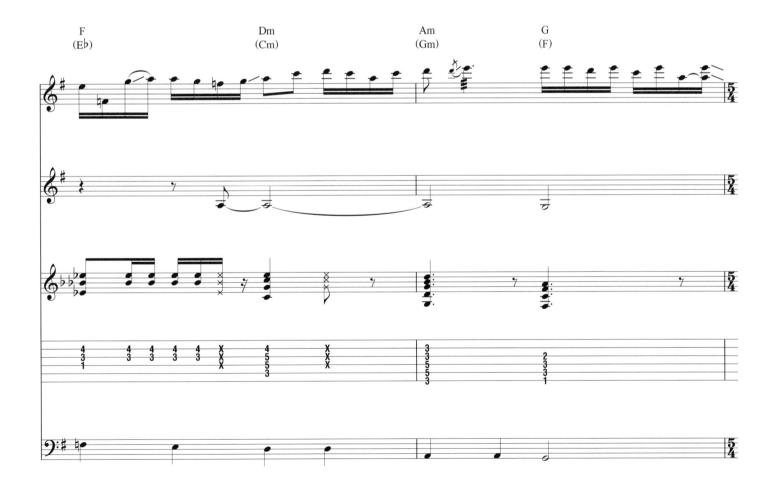

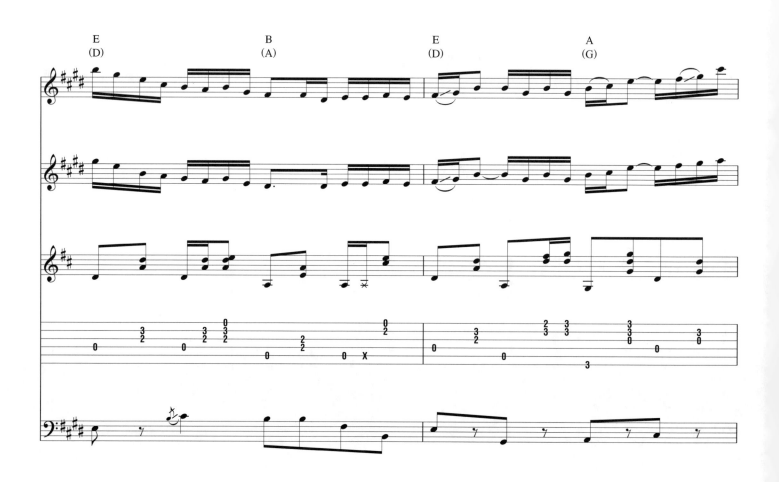

Arrange
whole
song

Anthony

Words and Music by Sara Watkins

Gtr. 1: Capo III
Ukulele tuning:
(low to high) F-Bb-D-G

Intro
Moderately ♩ = 116
Half-time feel

let ring - - - - - - - - - - - - - - - - - -

Verse

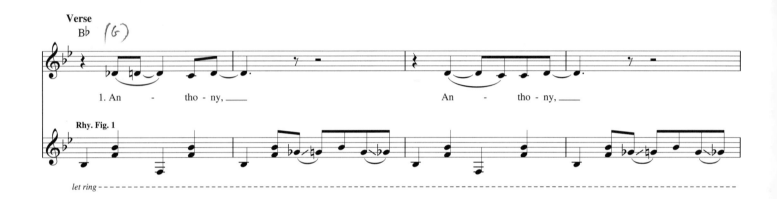

1. An - tho - ny, ____ An - tho - ny, ____

Rhy. Fig. 1

let ring - - - - - - - - - - - - -

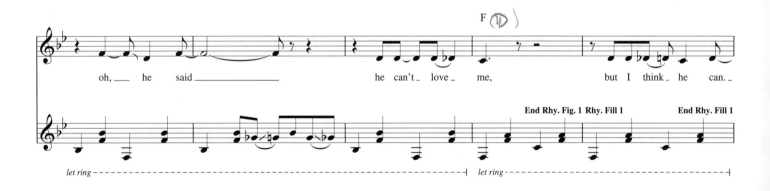

oh, ____ he said _____ he can't_ love_ me, ____ but I think_ he can.

End Rhy. Fig. 1   Rhy. Fill 1   End Rhy. Fill 1

let ring - - - - - - - - - - - - - - - - - - -   *let ring - - - - - - - - - - - - - - - - - -*

Ukulele: w/ Rhy. Fig. 1

____ Yes, I think ____ he can. ____

And I told ____ him that ____ just be - fore he ____ ran,

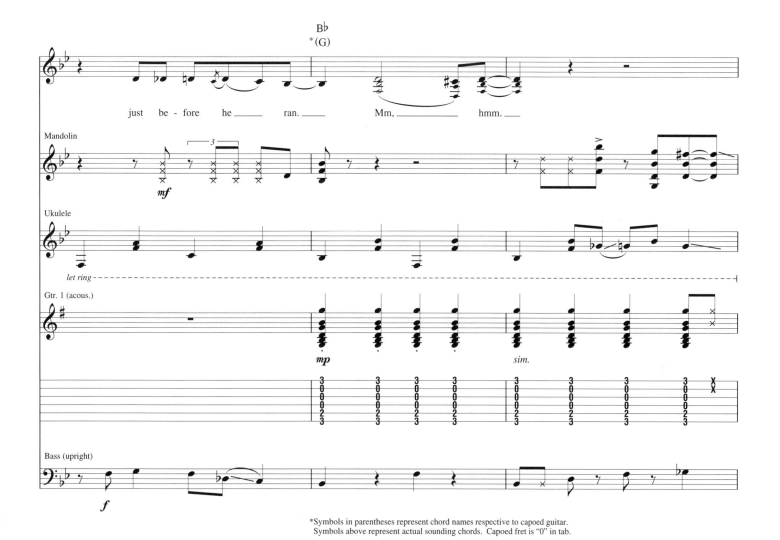

*Symbols in parentheses represent chord names respective to capoed guitar.
Symbols above represent actual sounding chords. Capoed fret is "0" in tab.

'cause he does - n't want ___

let ring –

End Rhy. Fig. 2

Ukulele: w/ Rhy. Fill 1

F
(D)

an - y - thing I have ___ or an - y - thing I ___ am. ___

let ring - - -┤   let ring - - - - -┤

Chorus

Ukulele: w/ Rhy. Fig. 1
Gtr. 1: w/ Rhy. Fig. 2

Best of Luck

Words and Music by Chris Thile, Sean Watkins and Sara Watkins

*Symbols in parentheses represent chord names respective to detuned guitar.
Symbols above reflect actual sounding chords.

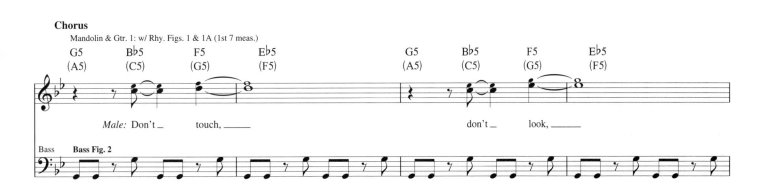

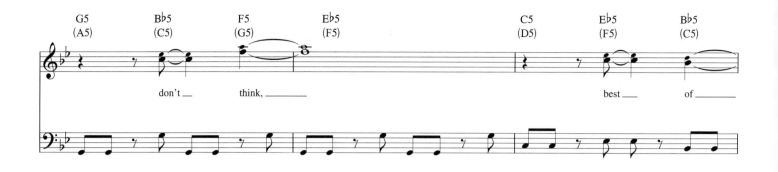

Verse

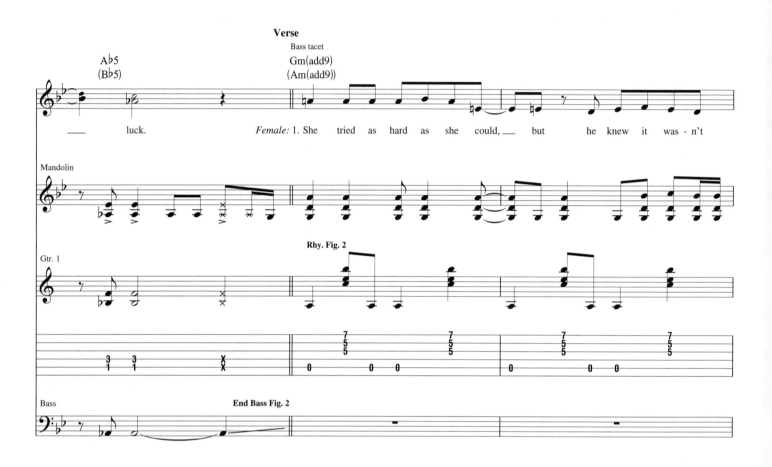

Verse

Both: 2. He's still shak-in' it off,____ buys flow-ers for his wife,____ guilt-y he could e-ven

*Lead Voc.: Female, Harmony Voc: Male

think of life with-out her. Gets home look-in' like he's seen a ghost. She's read-y for the

Chorus

Mandolin & Gtr. 1: w/ Rhy. Figs. 1 & 1A (1 5/8 times)
Bass: w/ Bass Fig. 2 (1 5/8 times)

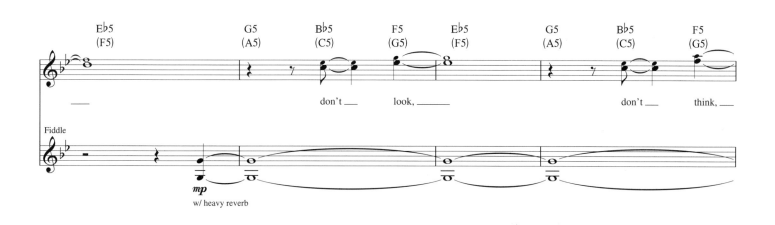

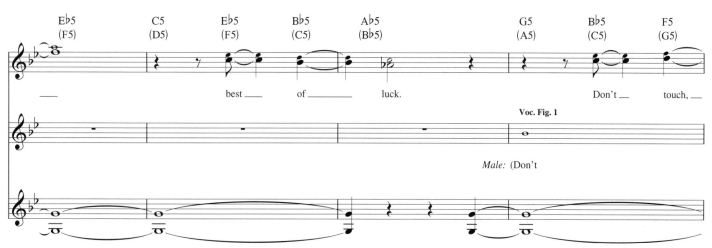

103

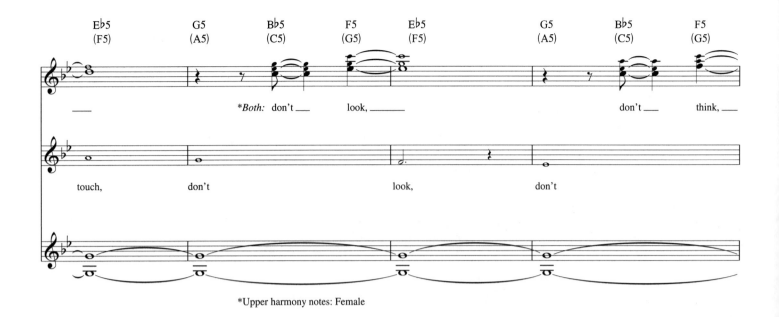

*Both: don't ___ look, ___ don't ___ think, ___

touch, don't look, don't

*Upper harmony notes: Female

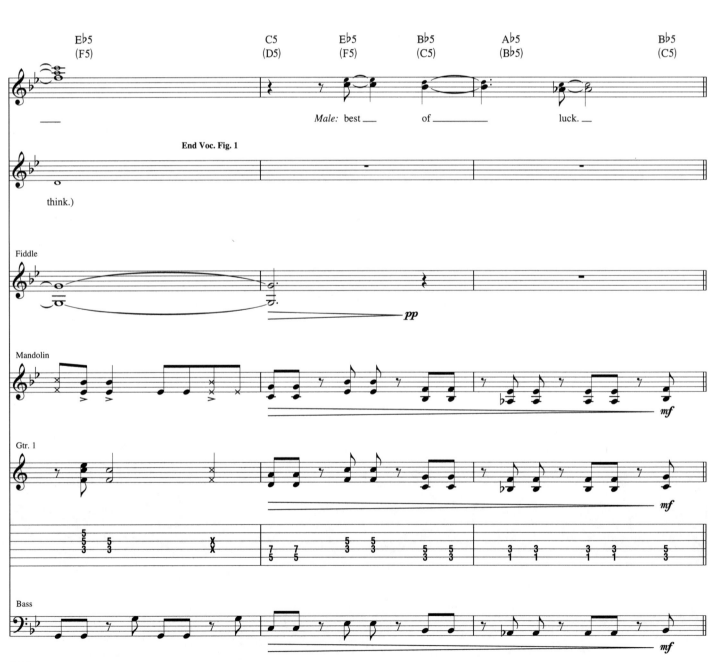

think.)

Male: best ___ of ___ luck. ___

End Voc. Fig. 1

Fiddle

pp

Mandolin

mf

Gtr. 1

mf

Bass

mf

Interlude

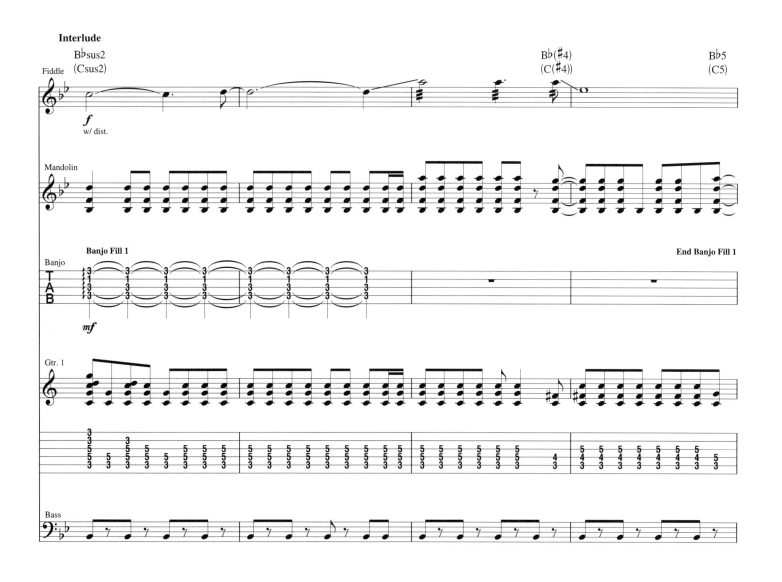

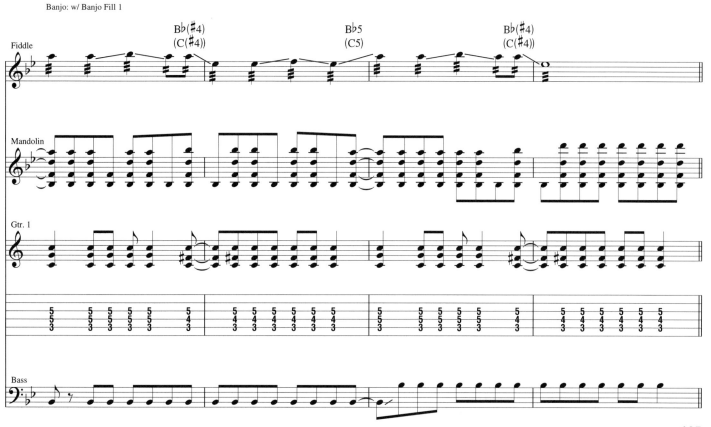

Verse

Female: 3. We did-n't want our __ love to end in high __ school. In col-lege I called ev-'ry day un-

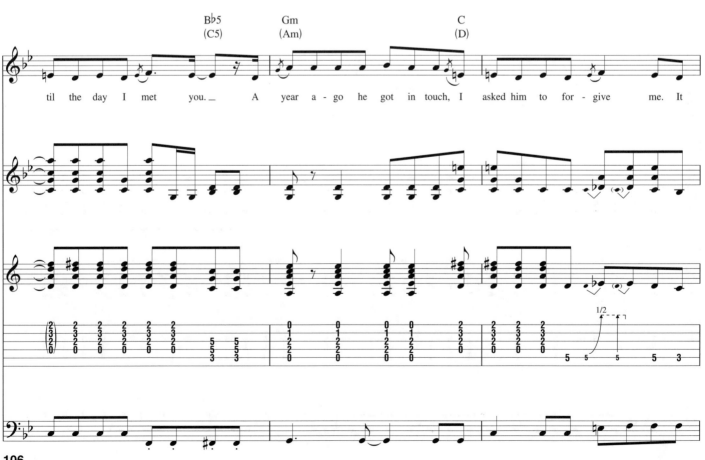

til the day I met you. __ A year a-go he got in touch, I asked him to for-give me. It

Chorus

Mandolin & Gtr. 1: w/ Rhy. Figs. 3 & 3A
Bass: w/ Bass Fig. 3

should-a end-ed there, but I for-got I was-n't eight - een. *Male:* Don't touch,

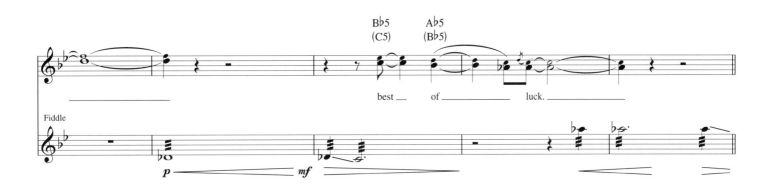

best of luck.

Fiddle

Verse

Mandolin & Gtr. 1: w/ Rhy. Figs. 4 & 4A
Bass: w/ Bass Fig. 4

Fiddle tacet

Both: 4. She'll try as hard as she can, but he'll know it is-n't good e-nough and won't ev-er

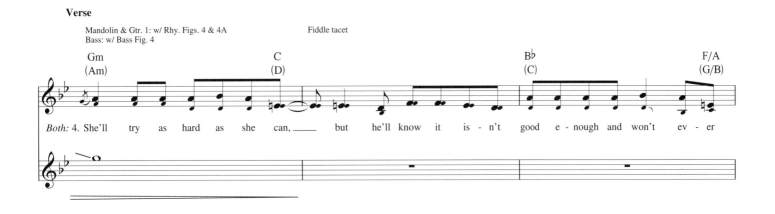

be. So she'll have to start hid-in' how she feels though she loves him and he knows it. Still, his

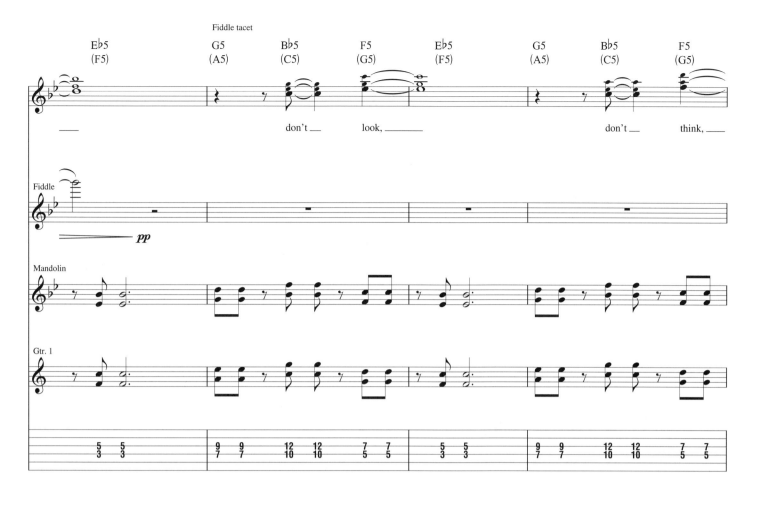

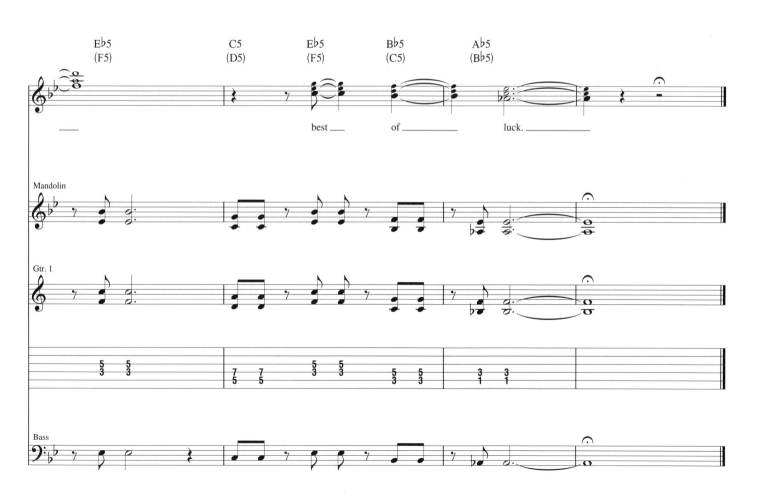

Doubting Thomas

Words and Music by Chris Thile

Gtr. 1: Tuning, Capo IV:
(low to high) D-A-E-F♯-A-E

Intro
Moderately slow ♩ = 74

*Symbols in parentheses represent chord names respective to capoed guitar.
Symbols above represent actual sounding chords. Capoed fret is "0" in tab.
Chord symbols reflect overall harmony.

Verse

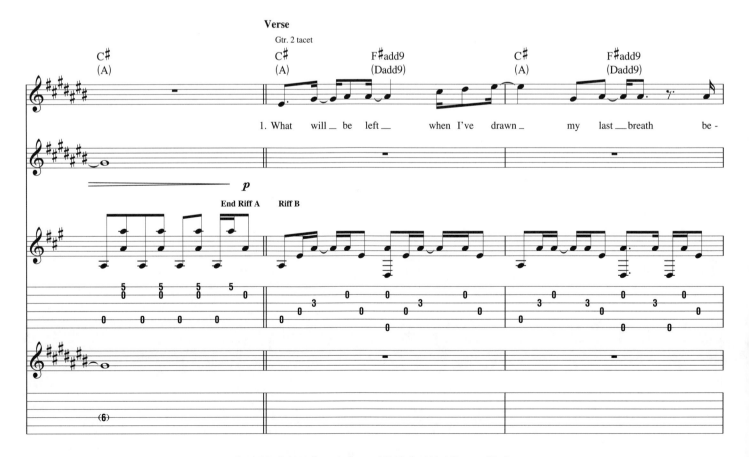

1. What will be left when I've drawn my last breath be-

sides the folks _ I've met _ and the folks _ who know _ me? Will I __ dis - cov - er a

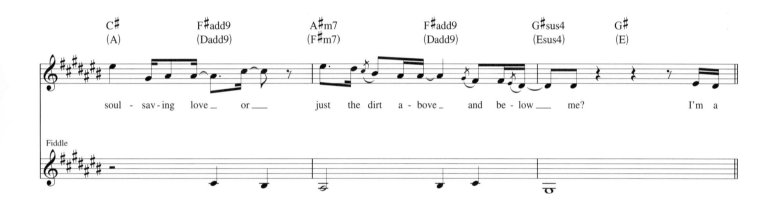

soul - sav - ing love _ or __ just the dirt a - bove _ and be - low __ me? I'm a

Chorus

doubt - ing Thom - as. I took a prom-ise but I __ do not __ feel _ safe. _

Oh, me of lit-tle faith.

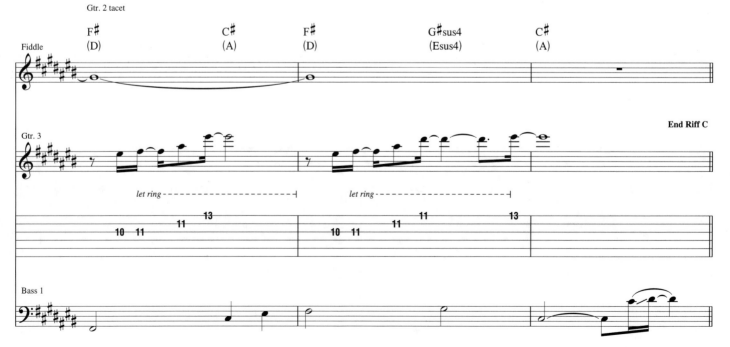

Verse

Gtr. 1: w/ Riff B (2 times)
Gtr. 2: w/ Rhy. Fig. 1 (4 times)
Gtr. 3 tacet

2. Some - times __ I pray __ for a slap __ in the face, __ then I beg __

to __ be spared __ 'cause I'm a cow - ard. If there's a

mas - ter __ of death, __ I'll bet he's hold - ing __ his breath __ as I show the blind __

and __ tell the deaf __ a - bout his pow - er. __ I'm a

113

Chorus

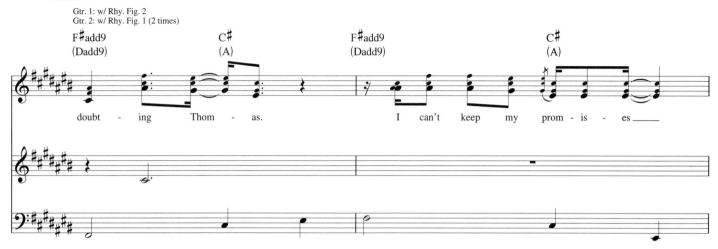

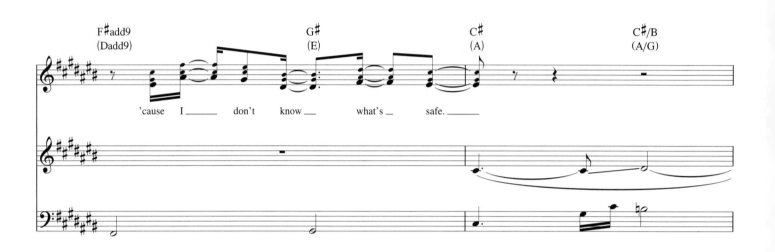

Chorus

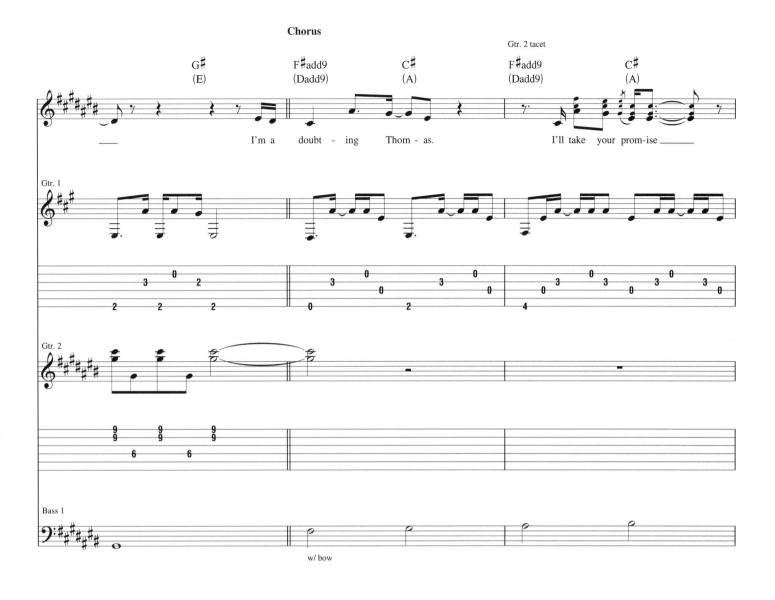

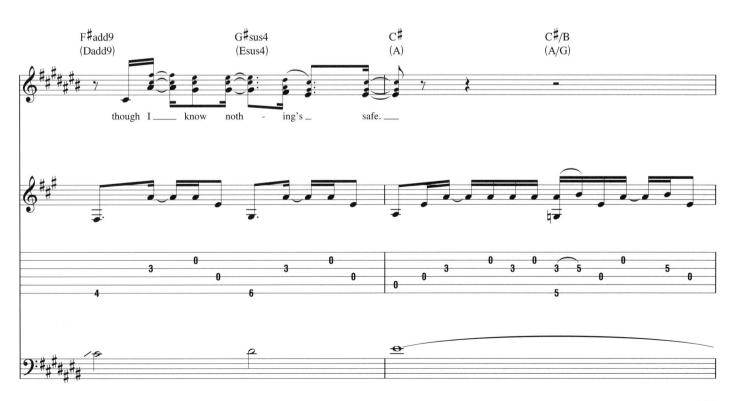

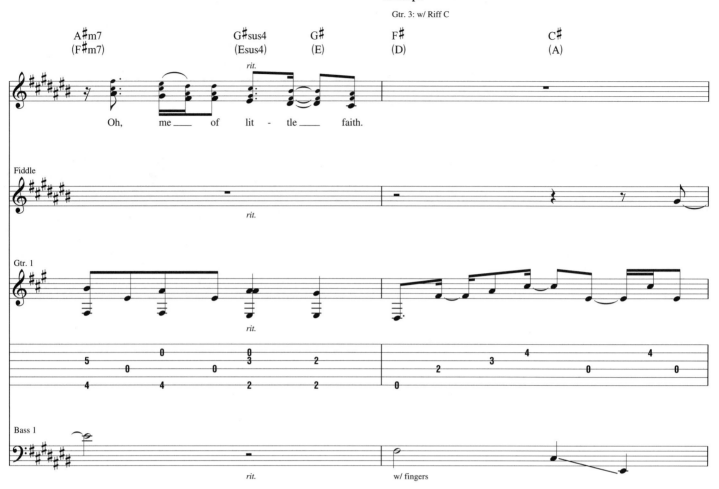

First and Last Waltz

By Chris Thile, Sean Watkins and Sara Watkins

*Chord symbols reflect overall harmony.

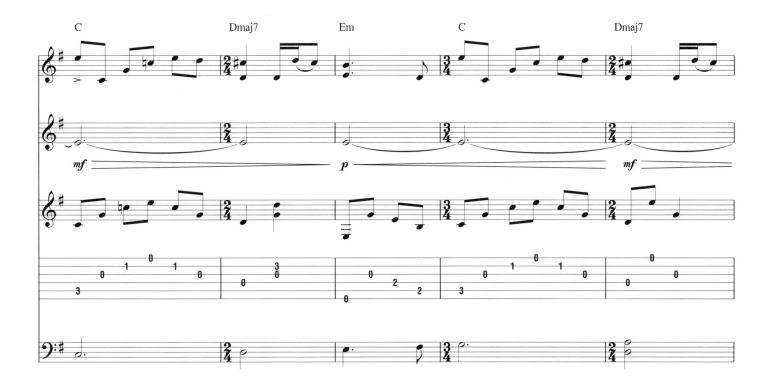

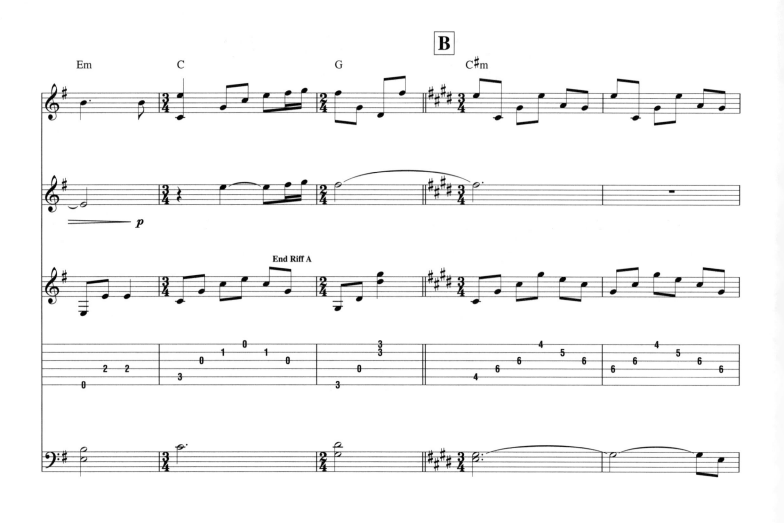

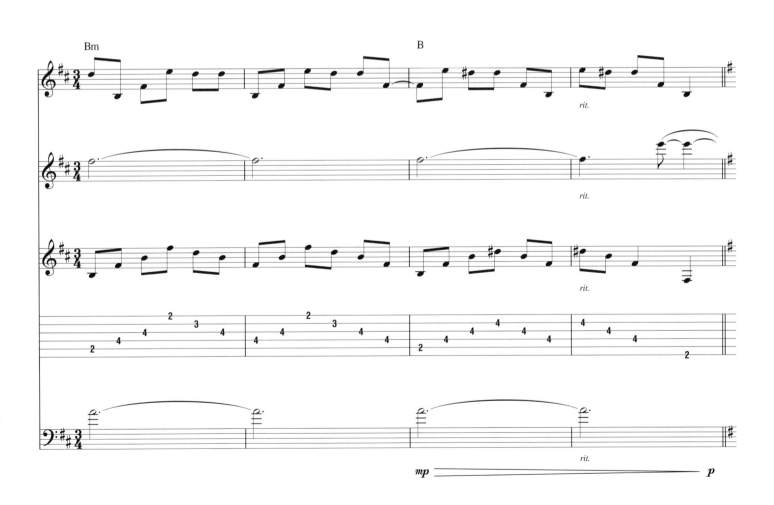

A tempo

Gtr. 1: w/ Riff A

Helena

Words and Music by Chris Thile

Gtr. 1 (Tenor gtr.) tuning:
(low to high) D-G-B-E

Verse
Moderately ♩ = 133

1. Hel - e - na, ___ don't walk ___ a - way ___ be - fore you give ___

___ me back my heart. If it ___ were ___

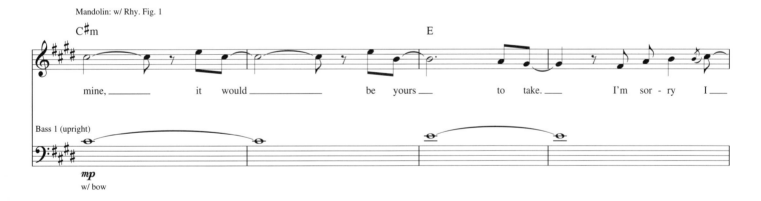

mine, ___ it would ___ be yours ___ to take. ___ I'm sor - ry I

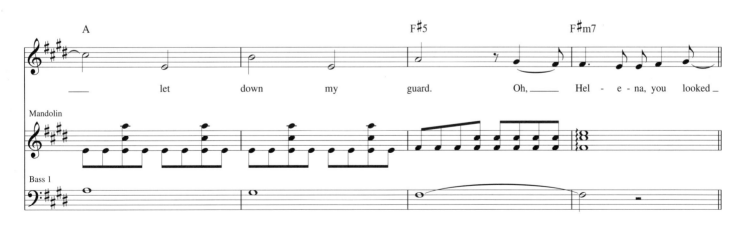

___ let down my guard. Oh, ___ Hel - e - na, you looked ___

Chorus

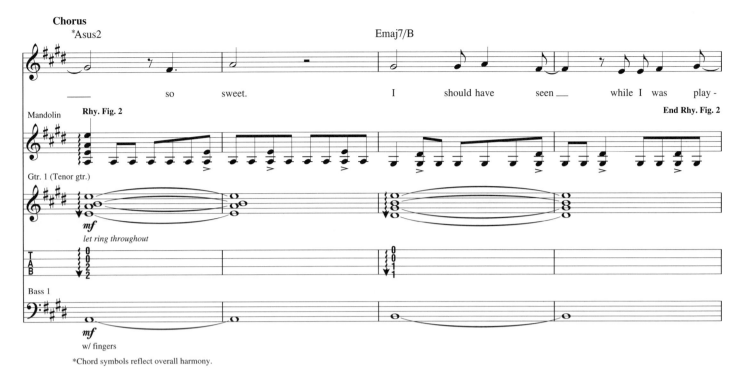

*Chord symbols reflect overall harmony.

Verse

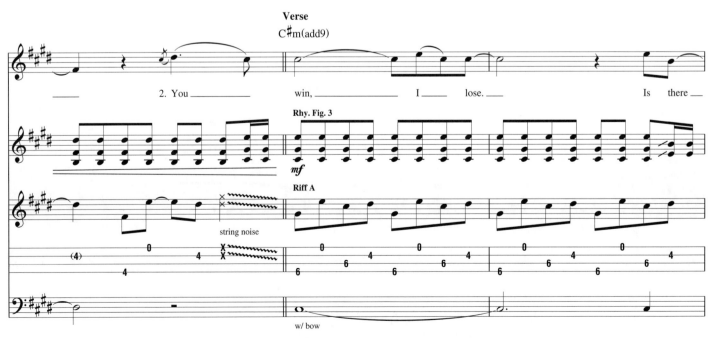

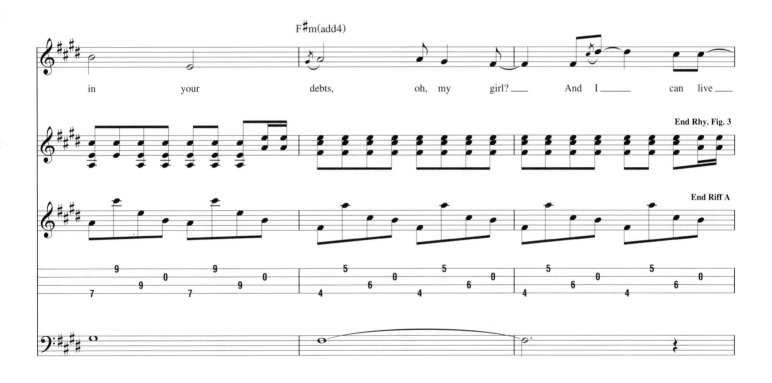

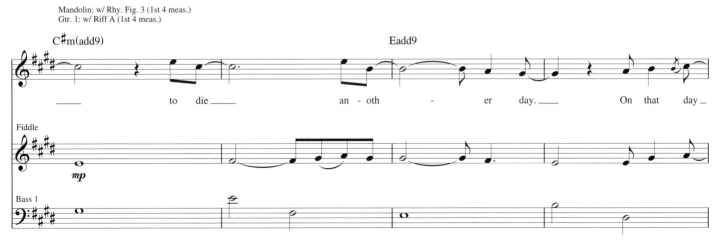

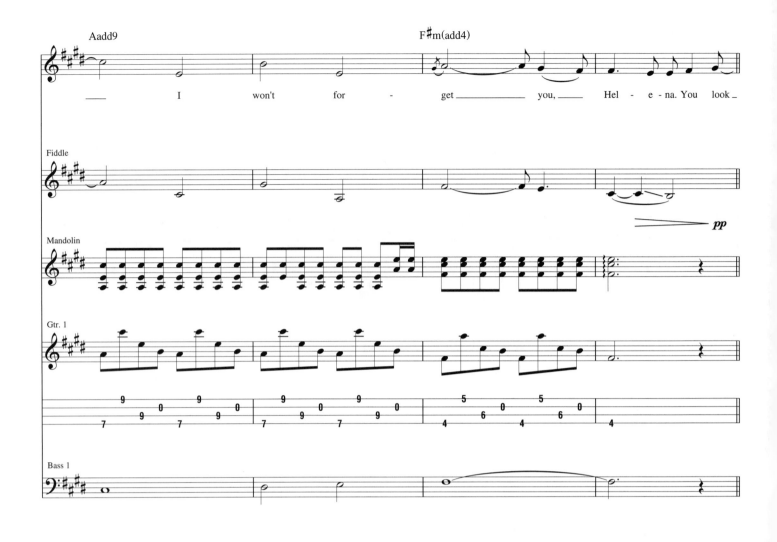

Chorus

for her ____ to give ____ me an-y rea - son ____ to leave. _

Don't _____ waste _____ your pret - ty

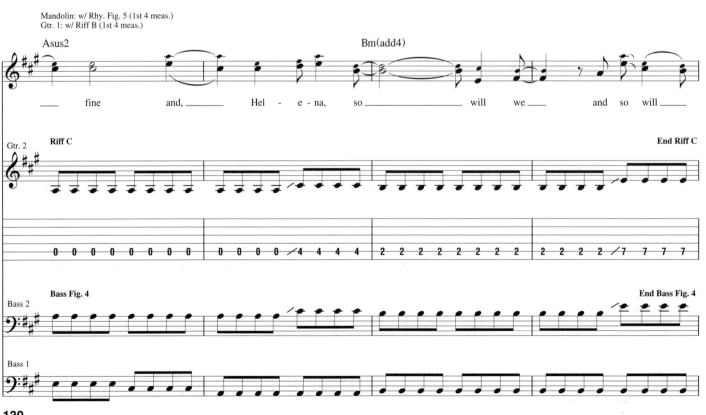

ev - 'ry - thing ___ in ___ time. ___ Mm. ___

Interlude

Mandolin: w/ Rhy. Fig. 3
Gtr. 1: w/ Riff A
Gtr. 2 & Bass 2 tacet

Verse

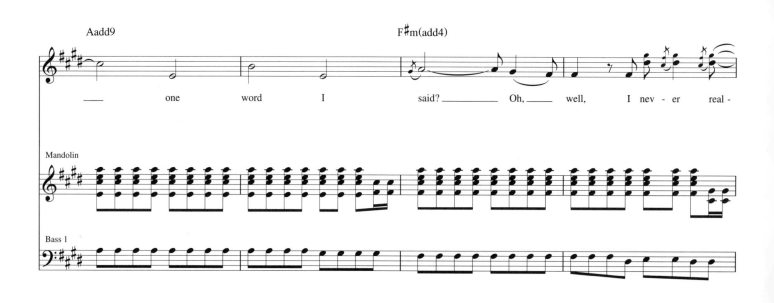

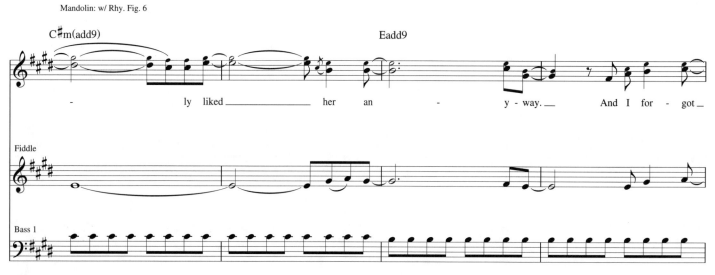

her; I'll for - get _____ you, Hel - e - na. You're not _____

Chorus

Fiddle tacet
Gtr. 1: w/ Rhy. Fig. 4
Bass 1: w/ Bass Fig. 1

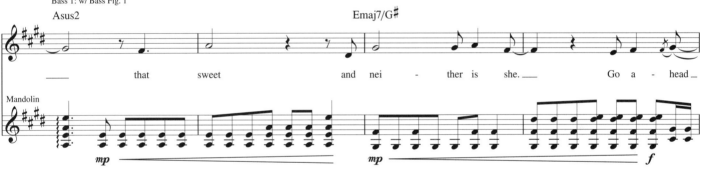

that sweet and nei - ther is she. _____ Go a - head _____

and tell _____ her an - y - thing. _____ You _____

Bridge

Mandolin: w/ Rhy. Fig. 5 (3 times)
Gtr. 1: w/ Riff B (2 4/6 times)
Gtr. 2: w/ Riff B1 (2 times)
Bass 1: w/ Bass Fig. 2
Bass 2: w/ Bass Fig. 3 (2 times)

_____ are good, _____ Hel - e - na. Guys _____ like me _____ nev - er

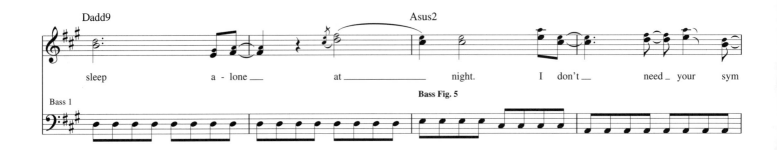

sleep   a - lone ___ at ___ night.   I don't ___ need ___ your   sym

Bass 1

Bass Fig. 5

- pa - thy ___ 'cause I'll ___ al - ways be ___ just ___

End Bass Fig. 5

Gtr. 2: w/ Riff C
Bass 1: w/ Bass Fig. 5
Bass 2: w/ Bass Fig. 4

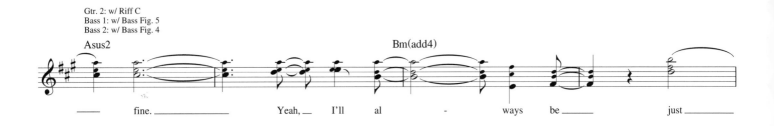

___ fine.   Yeah, ___ I'll   al - ways be ___ just ___

Outro

Mandolin: w/ Rhy. Fig. 5 (3 4/6 times)
Bass 1: w/ Bass Fig. 5 (3 4/6 times)

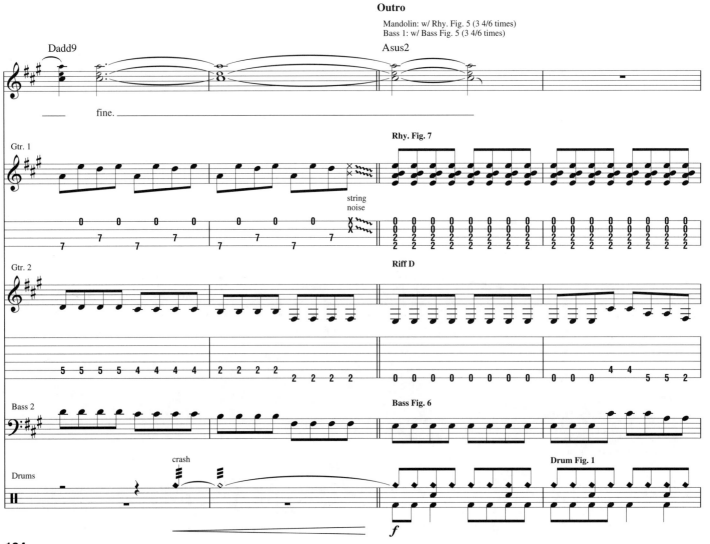

___ fine. ___

Rhy. Fig. 7

string
noise

Gtr. 2

Riff D

Bass 2

Bass Fig. 6

crash

Drums

Drum Fig. 1

f

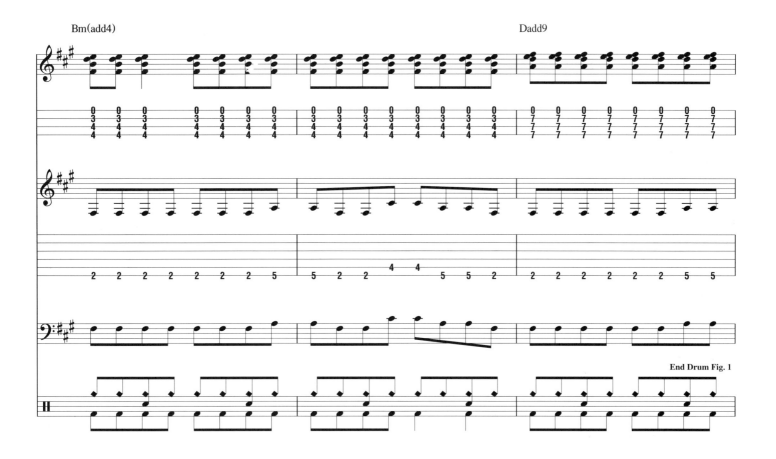

Drums: w/ Drum Fig. 1   Gtr. 1: w/ Rhy. Fig. 7 (2 4/6 times)

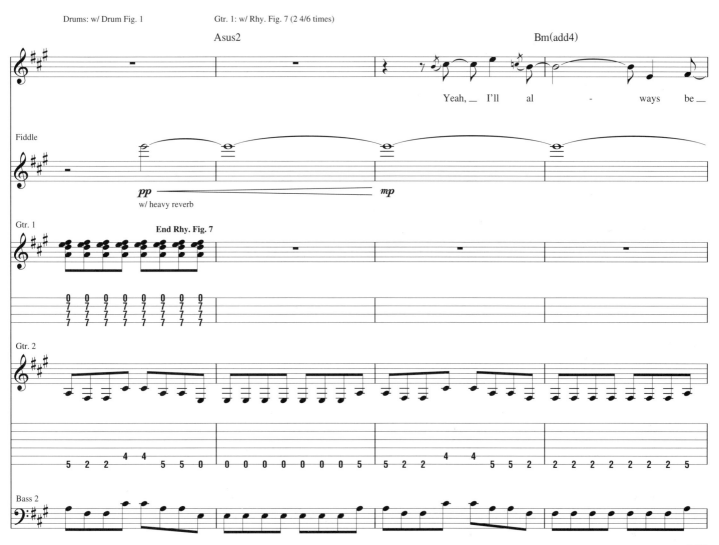

Yeah, __ I'll al - ways be __

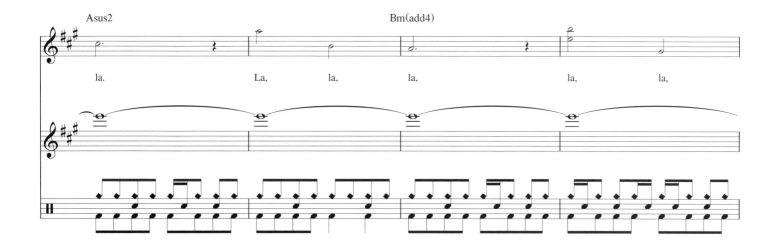

Why Should the Fire Die?

Words and Music by Chris Thile, Sean Watkins and Sara Watkins

Guitar Notation Legend

Guitar Music can be notated three different ways: on a *musical staff*, in *tablature*, and in *rhythm slashes*.

RHYTHM SLASHES are written above the staff. Strum chords in the rhythm indicated. Use the chord diagrams found at the top of the first page of the transcription for the appropriate chord voicings. Round noteheads indicate single notes.

THE MUSICAL STAFF shows pitches and rhythms and is divided by bar lines into measures. Pitches are named after the first seven letters of the alphabet.

TABLATURE graphically represents the guitar fingerboard. Each horizontal line represents a string, and each number represents a fret.

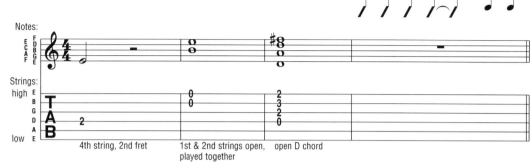

HALF-STEP BEND: Strike the note and bend up 1/2 step.

WHOLE-STEP BEND: Strike the note and bend up one step.

GRACE NOTE BEND: Strike the note and immediately bend up as indicated.

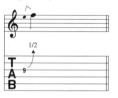

SLIGHT (MICROTONE) BEND: Strike the note and bend up 1/4 step.

BEND AND RELEASE: Strike the note and bend up as indicated, then release back to the original note. Only the first note is struck.

PRE-BEND: Bend the note as indicated, then strike it.

VIBRATO: The string is vibrated by rapidly bending and releasing the note with the fretting hand.

WIDE VIBRATO: The pitch is varied to a greater degree by vibrating with the fretting hand.

HAMMER-ON: Strike the first (lower) note with one finger, then sound the higher note (on the same string) with another finger by fretting it without picking.

PULL-OFF: Place both fingers on the notes to be sounded. Strike the first note and without picking, pull the finger off to sound the second (lower) note.

LEGATO SLIDE: Strike the first note and then slide the same fret-hand finger up or down to the second note. The second note is not struck.

SHIFT SLIDE: Same as legato slide, except the second note is struck.

TRILL: Very rapidly alternate between the notes indicated by continuously hammering on and pulling off.

TAPPING: Hammer ("tap") the fret indicated with the pick-hand index or middle finger and pull off to the note fretted by the fret hand.

NATURAL HARMONIC: Strike the note while the fret-hand lightly touches the string directly over the fret indicated.

PINCH HARMONIC: The note is fretted normally and a harmonic is produced by adding the edge of the thumb or the tip of the index finger of the pick hand to the normal pick attack.

PICK SCRAPE: The edge of the pick is rubbed down (or up) the string, producing a scratchy sound.

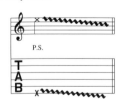

MUFFLED STRINGS: A percussive sound is produced by laying the fret hand across the string(s) without depressing, and striking them with the pick hand.

PALM MUTING: The note is partially muted by the pick hand lightly touching the string(s) just before the bridge.

RAKE: Drag the pick across the strings indicated with a single motion.

TREMOLO PICKING: The note is picked as rapidly and continuously as possible.

VIBRATO BAR DIVE AND RETURN: The pitch of the note or chord is dropped a specified number of steps (in rhythm) then returned to the original pitch.

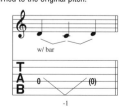

VIBRATO BAR SCOOP: Depress the bar just before striking the note, then quickly release the bar.

VIBRATO BAR DIP: Strike the note and then immediately drop a specified number of steps, then release back to the original pitch.

Transcribed Scores are vocal and instrumental arrangements of music from some of the greatest groups in music. These excellent publications feature transcribed parts for lead vocals, lead guitar, rhythm, guitar, bass, drums, and all of the various instruments used in each specific recording session. All songs are arranged exactly the way the artists recorded them.

Prices and availability subject to change

FOR MORE INFORMATION, SEE YOUR LOCAL MUSIC DEALER, OR WRITE TO:

HAL•LEONARD® CORPORATION
7777 W. BLUEMOUND RD. P.O. BOX 13819 MILWAUKEE, WI 53213

Visit Hal Leonard online at **www.halleonard.com**

0205